MW00959017

Becoming a Proverbs 31 Woman:
Learning to lose the intimidation

By: Amanda Peterson

Cover Art By: Sandra Steedle

Copyright © 2014 by Amanda R. Peterson

All rights reserved. This book or any portion thereof
may not be reproduced or used in any manner whatsoever
without the express written permission of the publisher
except for the use of brief quotations in a book review.

Printed in the United States of America

First Printing, 2014
ISBN-13: 978-1500614812
ISBN-10: 1500614815

Amanda Peterson
amandap3311@gmail.com
www.amandarpeterson.blogspot.com

Dedication

To my weekly Bible study ladies Aimee, Dawn, and Liz who went through this with me first. Your willingness to learn about the Lord inspires me every day.

Table of Contents

Introduction 1

Chapter 1: A Woman Who Fears the Lord 5

Chapter 2: A Self-Controlled and Virtuous Woman 23

Chapter 3: A Responsible Woman 39

Chapter 4: A Kind and Compassionate Woman 57

Chapter 5: A Hardworking and Resourceful Woman 75

Chapter 6: An Energetic Woman 93

Chapter 7: A Wise Woman 113

Chapter 8: A Loved Woman 135

Wrapping it Up 155

Introduction

Proverbs 31 has been a favorite topic of Bible studies for years. We hear sermons on it for Mother's day, dig into it in a Bible class, or participate in a Ladies Day centered on it. There's something special about the Proverbs 31 Woman. We look at her and see a perfect example of womanhood – someone we might hope to live up to while being horribly intimidated by her at the same time. We want to emulate her, but we always fall short. No one is that perfect, right?

With this study I'm hoping to explore the proverb and the woman it's about in a different way. I've gone through the Proverb from beginning to end many times, and I've pulled out character traits about the Proverbs 31 Woman that seem to recur throughout the passage. You see, this woman is more than a pretty poem – she is a wonderful example for Christian ladies today. We can read all about her attributes in this proverb and learn how to adapt her characteristics. None of us will do it perfectly, but let's face it, neither did she. We don't read about her bad days and failures in the proverb; we read about her successes and the legacy she gave her family. That's certainly something we can aspire to in our lives, isn't it?

I hope that you will endeavor to take the lessons from this book to heart as you read and study. My goal with this book is for you to develop a closer relationship with God, your family, and your Christian sisters. I hope you will learn to look for these characteristics in yourself and other Christians around you.

Group Brainstorming

Group Goals

What would you like to see your group accomplish during the course of this study?

What can we be praying for as a group?

Personal Goals

What are you personally looking for from this study?

What area(s) of your life do you need God's help with?

What struggles are you having as a wife, mother, and woman that you want this study to help with?

Proverbs 31

Sayings of King Lemuel

The sayings of King Lemuel--an oracle his mother taught him: "O my son, O son of my womb, O son of my vows, do not spend your strength on women, your vigor on those who ruin kings. "It is not for kings, O Lemuel-- not for kings to drink wine, not for rulers to crave beer, lest they drink and forget what the law decrees, and deprive all the oppressed of their rights. Give beer to those who are perishing, wine to those who are in anguish; let them drink and forget their poverty and remember their misery no more. "Speak up for those who cannot speak for themselves, for the rights of all who are destitute. Speak up and judge fairly; defend the rights of the poor and needy."

Epilogue: The Wife of Noble Character

A wife of noble character who can find? She is worth far more than rubies. Her husband has full confidence in her and lacks nothing of value. She brings him good, not harm, all the days of her life. She selects wool and flax and works with eager hands. She is like the merchant ships, bringing her food from afar. She gets up while it is still dark; she provides food for her family and portions for her servant girls. She considers a field and buys it; out of her earnings she plants a vineyard. She sets about her work vigorously; her arms are strong for her tasks. She sees that her trading is profitable, and her lamp does not go out at night. In her hand she holds the distaff and grasps the spindle with her fingers. She opens her arms to the poor and extends her hands to the needy. When it snows, she has no fear for her household; for all of them are clothed in scarlet. She makes coverings for her bed; she is clothed in fine linen and purple. Her husband is respected at the city gate, where he takes his seat among the elders of the land. She makes linen garments and sells them, and supplies the merchants with sashes. She is clothed with strength and dignity; she can laugh at the days to come. She speaks with wisdom, and faithful instruction is on her tongue. She watches over the affairs of her household and does not eat the bread of idleness. Her children arise and call her blessed; her husband also, and he praises her: "Many women do noble things, but you surpass them all." Charm is deceptive, and beauty is fleeting; but a woman who fears the LORD is to be praised. Give her the reward she has earned, and let her works bring her praise at the city gate.

Chapter 1
A Woman Who Fears the Lord

Objective: In this lesson we will learn what fear of the Lord means to each one of us and develop a closer relationship to God through understanding and applying the concept.

The Fear of the Lord

What an ominous sounding phrase. What does it mean? Does it mean we approach God with trembling knees and shaking voices, fearing what he may do to us at any moment? Does it mean we live our lives in constant fear of making a mistake and being condemned forever? There are so many questions this topic raises for many of us, and sometimes the answers can seem hard to find.

It's important to understand what fear we are talking about. This isn't the shivery creepy fear that we see in scary movies or the terror that we feel when we're scared. Fear of the Lord is something completely different and life-changing. Fear of the Lord is reverent awe, respect, and honor. Have you ever felt that for someone? Maybe you've met a famous person you've always looked up to. You revere them and find yourself showing them respect – you may not know what to say to them because you're so awe-struck.

This is how you should feel when you approach God. We should be His ultimate "fan-girls!" That reverent fear should be the foundation of everything we believe about God. With fear of the Lord as your foundation, think of all the things you can do for God.

Definitions

Fear (as a verb) has four main definitions:

1. *archaic* : <u>frighten</u>
2. *archaic* : to feel fear in (oneself)
3. to have a reverential awe of <*fear* God>
4. to be afraid of : expect with alarm <*fear* the worst>

(http://www.merriam-webster.com/dictionary/fear)

Bible dictionaries are also a handy resource for this topic because they help us determine the original words used by the Bible authors.

According to Old Testament Hebrew Lexicon, the Hebrew word **yaré** translates as:*" to fear, revere, be afraid (Qal) to fear, be afraid to stand in awe of, be awed to fear, reverence, honour, respect (Niphal) to be fearful, be dreadful, be feared to cause astonishment and awe, be held in awe to inspire reverence or godly fear or awe (Piel) to make afraid, terrify."* (www.biblestudytools.com)

What does that mean? It means we should approach the Lord with awe, respect, and love, always being mindful of his awesome power, mighty wrath for sin, and all-encompassing grace and love for those covered by the blood of Jesus. We all have every reason to fear God; if we had to face Him by our own merits alone, we would be lost forever. We, as humans, can never measure up to the perfection of our God. That is why He sent His Son to us. It's through Jesus that our frightened fear becomes reverent fear and awe for His power.

This doesn't mean that we approach God casually and assume all is forgiven. Reverent fear means that we are fully aware of what we deserve from God and fully aware of His power and greatness. We acknowledge that we are sinners and worthless without Christ, and we acknowledge that we are lost without Him. When we approach God with reverent fear, it means we come to Him with a humble, open heart and ultimate respect for all He's done for us.

As we study the Proverbs 31 Woman, it is important for us to remember that in everything she does she fears the Lord. It's this obedience to him that allows her to be so successful. It overrides every part of her life and every moment of her day. She's not a perfect person – none of us are. I'm sure she has faults and bad days just like the rest of us. We look at this Proverb and often think, "That's not attainable. There's no way I can do all the stuff she does. It's just not possible." We need to learn how to replace that doubt with confidence: confidence that through God we can attain these attributes and grow into modern-day Proverbs 31 women. What we need to focus on first is the foundation of everything she does – fearing the Lord.

What is so important about a foundation? As homeowners know, the key to a strong building is a strong foundation. If your foundation is faulty, your home may very well come crumbling down around you at any moment. Fear of the Lord is a foundational issue for us as Christians. Without that reverent fear and respect, we have a skewed vision of God and His purpose in our lives. If He isn't the all-powerful, omniscient Creator of the Universe, why do we need to follow Him and do what He says? When we make that fear of God and belief in the truth of Him and His word our foundation, we can begin to grow and thrive.

Proverbs 31:30

Charm is deceptive, and beauty is fleeting; but a woman who fears the LORD is to be praised. (NIV)

What is this verse talking about?

What does this verse teach you about the importance of fearing the Lord?

Why are charm and beauty fleeting and deceptive?

How many times have you read this verse and ignored the second half? We love to focus on the first phrase, *"Charm is deceptive, and beauty is fleeting..."* as if that's all there is to this verse. Why do we forget the most important part, *"But a woman who fears the Lord is to be praised?"* While I agree that we shouldn't focus on outward appearance and superficial personality traits, this verse is teaching us that fearing the Lord is more important than anything we can manufacture on our own.

We don't have to be beautiful or witty to be praised as a strong woman for Christ. That should be comforting to all of us. God doesn't care if you spent the day in your pajamas or covered in spit up. He is looking right into your heart and soul, and He knows what your foundation is. He can tell if you have placed Him at the foundation of your beliefs or if you are leaning on your own wisdom and understanding and trying to hide your true self from Him and others.

How many people do you know who rely on their outward appearance or their sparkling personality to hide their true character? I'm sure we can all point out various Hollywood actors who look good on the outside, but inside are hollow, tortured souls desperately searching for something. Do you realize how blessed we are to have God as our foundation? We have no hollow place inside when we fear the Lord. He will fill all our empty spaces with His love and wisdom. I don't know about you, but I would much rather have my average face and God as my foundation than a pretty face and empty soul.

He's ready and willing to fill our empty spaces. How many times does He call out to us in Scripture? We have to make that choice – God or the world? What foundation are you going to stand on?

Psalm 19

The heavens declare the glory of God; the skies proclaim the work of his hands. Day after day they pour forth speech; night after night they display knowledge. There is no speech or language where their voice is not heard. Their voice goes out into all the earth, their words to the ends of the world. In the heavens he has pitched a tent for the sun, which is like a bridegroom coming forth from his pavilion, like a champion rejoicing to run his course. It rises at one end of the heavens and makes its circuit to the other; nothing is hidden from its heat. The law of the LORD is perfect, reviving the soul. The statutes of the LORD are trustworthy, making wise the simple. The precepts of the LORD are right, giving joy to the heart. The commands of the LORD are radiant, giving light to the eyes. The fear of the LORD is pure, enduring forever. The ordinances of the LORD are sure and altogether righteous. They are more precious than gold, than much pure gold; they are sweeter than honey, than honey from the comb. By them is your servant warned; in keeping them there is great reward. Who can discern his errors? Forgive my hidden faults. Keep your servant also from willful sins; may they not rule over me. Then will I be blameless, innocent of great transgression. May the words of my mouth and the meditation of my heart be pleasing in your sight, O LORD, my Rock and my Redeemer. (NIV)

What images does this psalm evoke in your mind?

What does the psalm tell you about fearing the Lord?

In terms of your life today, how can this psalm help you?

Are there any phrases or verses that particularly speak to you?

When I read this psalm, I feel the awe and love the psalmist has for God. This is one of David's psalms, and I think it gives us a good idea of how David felt about God. It paints such a beautiful picture of the awesomeness of God and the sheer joy found in serving him. This to me seems to be an overflowing of the David's soul – he can't contain his love and excitement about God.

This is a great example of fearing the Lord. Have you ever felt that awe for God? Does your soul ever overflow with praise for Him? A woman who fears the Lord loves serving him and goes about it in such a way as to please him every day. Isn't it interesting that David describes the fear of the Lord as pure and enduring forever? There is nothing more pure than belief in and reliance on the perfect Creator of the universe. He also gives us a detailed description of God's ordinances (laws) and the wonder we find in following them. Have you ever thought of following God as something beautiful or precious? Do you search out His law like you would a hidden treasure? Think of the treasure that awaits you as a woman who fears the Lord.

Does this mean every day will be sunshine and roses for you if you fear the Lord? Of course not. We live in an imperfect world with imperfect people. Bad days are going to happen, and our lives will never be perfect. We can be assured of God's presence with us through everything we encounter. Look at what David ends the psalm with *"May the words of my mouth and the meditation of my heart be pleasing in your sight, O LORD, my Rock and my Redeemer."*

You are never alone in this world. If you spend your time trying to discern what is pleasing to God and striving to live for Him, you won't be disappointed at the result. He will be right there with you on the good days and the bad. We have the same Rock and Redeemer that David so profoundly wrote of right here with us every day.

Psalm 34

I will extol the LORD at all times; his praise will always be on my lips. My soul will boast in the LORD; let the afflicted hear and rejoice. Glorify the LORD with me; let us exalt his name together. I sought the LORD, and he answered me; he delivered me from all my fears. Those who look to him are radiant; their faces are never covered with shame. This poor man called, and the LORD heard him; he saved him out of all his troubles. The angel of the LORD encamps around those who fear him, and he delivers them. Taste and see that the LORD is good; blessed is the man who takes refuge in him. Fear the LORD, you his saints, for those who fear him lack nothing. The lions may grow weak and hungry, but those who seek the LORD lack no good thing. Come, my children, listen to me; I will teach you the fear of the LORD. Whoever of you loves life and desires to see many good days, keep your tongue from evil and your lips from speaking lies. Turn from evil and do good; seek peace and pursue it. The eyes of the LORD are on the righteous and his ears are attentive to their cry; the face of the LORD is against those who do evil, to cut off the memory of them from the earth. The righteous cry out, and the LORD hears them; he delivers them from all their troubles. The LORD is close to the brokenhearted and saves those who are crushed in spirit. A righteous man may have many troubles, but the LORD delivers him from them all; he protects all his bones, not one of them will be broken. Evil will slay the wicked; the foes of the righteous will be condemned. The LORD redeems his servants; no one will be condemned who takes refuge in him. (NIV)

Explain what verse 9 (*Fear the LORD, you his saints, for those who fear him lack nothing*) **means to you. Feel free to use the context of the psalm to help you. Does this mean that nothing bad will ever happen to you as a Christian?**

How does the psalmist describe fear of the Lord? How will he teach it? What are the requirements for those who fear the Lord?

I find a lot of comfort in this psalm. The Lord is telling us that we are never alone. He never promises us a perfect life, but he promises us that his arms will envelop us through any hardship we ever go through. I don't know about you, but I need to read this; better yet, I feel I need to absorb this psalm into my soul. What a comfort and peace our Lord offers to us if we just reach out and accept it from him. It sounds so easy, doesn't it?

I find it's easy to keep these things in the forefront of my mind while I'm reading them – it doesn't get hard to follow until life gets in the way and something bad happens. Lucy Q. from down the street says something rude…The dishwasher breaks…The car needs new tires…The kids need new shoes…A friend or family member gets cancer…That promotion your husband was counting on doesn't come through. These are all things that trip us up and can send us hurtling further from God and closer to self-doubt, anger, fear, and frustration. What do we do? How do we change? How do we learn to look at these things and not see disaster looming around the corner?

Go back and read the psalm again. What does God have to say about our troubles?

Is there anything in this psalm that will help you become a woman who fears the Lord?

Was there anything that this psalm made clearer to you?

Was there anything that confused the issue for you?

Wouldn't it be nice if being a Christian meant that your life was perfect? You would always be happy and content; life would be roses and flowers and puppies with no tears or negativity. I have run into Christians in my life who believe this way, and they always end up hurt and disappointed by life and the world around them.

You see, God doesn't promise perfection in this world. Perfection belongs to God, and we will only find it when we get to heaven someday. Here on earth we have been promised hardship and struggle, especially those of us who choose Christ. Why else would David talk about the righteous being persecuted and delivered by God? From early on, those of us who choose God choose a tough path – we're not the cool kids on the block – but it's a path that leads to ultimate salvation and eternal life in the presence of God.

As women who fear the Lord, we have to remember where our focus lies – on God and His eternal promises. Look again at what verses 7 through 9 say:
"The angel of the LORD encamps around those who fear him, and he delivers them. Taste and see that the LORD is good; blessed is the man who takes refuge in him. Fear the LORD, you his saints, for those who fear him lack nothing."

Fear the Lord, and He will protect you. You will lack nothing. That seems like a strong argument for fearing the Lord to me. Do you want to be complete and safe? Fear the Lord. Do you want blessings? Take refuge in Him. Let Him fold you in His arms every day. Let Him bless you in all that you do.

Proverbs 16:1-9

To man belong the plans of the heart, but from the LORD comes the reply of the tongue. All a man's ways seem innocent to him, but motives are weighed by the LORD. Commit to the LORD whatever you do, and your plans will succeed. The LORD works out everything for his own ends-- even the wicked for a day of disaster. The LORD detests all the proud of heart. Be sure of this: They will not go unpunished. Through love and faithfulness sin is atoned for; through the fear of the LORD a man avoids evil. When a man's ways are pleasing to the LORD, he makes even his enemies live at peace with him. Better a little with righteousness than much gain with injustice. In his heart a man plans his course, but the LORD determines his steps. (NIV)

What does this passage say to you?

What is the message here?

What do we learn about fearing the Lord?

Do you see the underlying theme to this passage? God has everything under control! What he's saying is we can plan and scheme all day long, but if our motives are not with Him, we will not succeed. If we set our hearts on Him and following His Word, we will succeed. If our hearts are set on Him, we will show Him the reverence, respect, and awe that He deserves as our Creator.

We *can* be women who fear the Lord. It's a conscious decision we have to make each day. It's not a guarantee that our lives will be perfect, or that we will be perfect. But it is a promise that God will be at our side every step we take.

Do you ever feel like you are helpless against evil? I find it interesting that fear of the Lord is one of our strongest weapons against evil. By making God your foundation, you can avoid evil in your life. Have you found this to be true? Think about your life before God – how did you stand up against evil then? Do you see how important a foundation of fearing God is? With God as our foundation, we will prevail. He will be there to catch us when we fall, He will pick us up when we are weak, He will carry us through our darkest hours.

If we decide to replace that foundation with something else we will be punished. We've all seen it – and maybe lived it – friends or loved ones who have replaced their "God" foundation with a worldly foundation. It's hard to see, especially when troubles come. How often does trouble destroy them when it comes their way? When you trade in fear of the Lord for belief in the world, what is there to sustain you or comfort you in your pain? Nothing. There is nothing for you outside of the Lord. No earthly teacher is going to sustain you the way God will. Fear Him, and let Him teach you. Let Him wrap His arms around you and walk through life with you.

Philippians 2:12-16

Therefore, my dear friends, as you have always obeyed--not only in my presence, but now much more in my absence--continue to work out your salvation with fear and trembling, for it is God who works in you to will and to act according to his good purpose. Do everything without complaining or arguing, so that you may become blameless and pure, children of God without fault in a crooked and depraved generation, in which you shine like stars in the universe as you hold out the word of life--in order that I may boast on the day of Christ that I did not run or labor for nothing. (NIV)

What is Paul's message to us here?

Why are we to work out our salvation with fear and trembling?

How do we become blameless and pure children of God?

Do you want to be known as someone who God works through? What kind of legacy would that be? I would love for people to see God working through my life. It's empowering to think about, isn't it? But stop and think for a minute about what that means for each of us. For God to work, we have to submit to His will and purpose. Look at what He requires from us: no complaints or arguments, faultless, fearless with the word of God. Over all of this we have to remember who saved us and what He saved us from. We should each get down on our knees to thank Him every day for the blessings He has given us. Thinking about God and what He has done for us should cause us to tremble. Does it? Does thinking about the sacrifice that Jesus made for you on the cross make you stop and think? Does it make you live differently?

Our foundation defines us as Christians. If your foundation is fear of the Lord, the rest will come. When God is your foundation, it gets easier to be kind to others and less scary to share the good news with friends and family. If you don't know what your foundation is, it's definitely time to get down on your knees and pray. Let God fill you up and make you shine like the stars!

Concluding Remarks

What I want you to take away from this lesson is this simple message: God, the creator of the universe, the maker of everything, the beginning and the end, loves *you*. He knows everything about you, and he loves you anyway. He contains all the power of the universe in his hands, and yet he is still concerned about your struggles and hardships, tears and laughter. If you give everything you are over to him – recognize his all-consuming power and his wrath for sin – He will bless you and never leave you. This is what our Proverbs 31 lady knows in her heart. She accepted his incredible gift.

Will you?

Challenge

Think about what you have learned about fearing the Lord so far.
**What are your challenges with this topic? Write down any areas
in which you may be struggling in fearing the Lord.**

Chapter 2
A Self-Controlled and
Virtuous Woman

Objective: To learn what it means to be a self-controlled and virtuous woman and how to accomplish it in our lives. Break down our preconceived notions about virtue and self-control, and find scripture that will teach the true meaning of each concept. Learn how we can get better at showing these characteristics in our lives.

Self-Control and Virtue

You're probably thinking I'm a little crazy to be putting these two things together in a study for grown women. Aren't these things we talk to teenagers about when they start dating? Isn't virtue something that went out of vogue when knights put up their swords? What image pops into your head when you think of a self-controlled person? Probably someone who's serious and no fun to be around – someone who wouldn't be caught dead cracking a joke or having fun.

What does this have to do with women today, and what does it have to do with the Proverbs 31 Woman we're learning about? Do you ever think of self-control or virtue as it relates to your walk as a Christian? Maybe it's time that we do. Virtue is just as important today as it was in Jesus' time. Likewise, self-control is necessary for anyone who wants to walk a successful path as a Christian. Our culture teaches us that self-control and virtue are antiquated and unnecessary in today's world. As Christians it's our job to know that our culture is wrong in this thinking.

We're going to look at how we can become self-controlled, virtuous women and *why* we want to do that. I think you will agree with me that the Proverbs 31 Woman exhibited both of these characteristics in the passage we have read.

However, I think sometimes we get lost in all the things she can do, all the characteristics she possesses, and we automatically assume we're going to be lacking in all the areas talked about. But it doesn't have to be that way. Remember that she is not a perfect woman and neither are we. None of us are – thus the need for Jesus and his saving power. Take comfort in this fact. If she, as an imperfect woman, can master these things, then so can we!

Definitions

Let's break down each of these terms and see what they actually mean.

According to Merriam-Webster online **self-control** is defined as: restraint exercised over one's own impulses, emotions, or desires. (www.merriam-webster.com/dictionary/self-control)

Virtue has more definitions:
1. a : conformity to a standard of right : morality
2. b : a particular moral excellence
3. plural : an order of angels — see celestial hierarchy
4. : a beneficial quality or power of a thing
5. : manly strength or courage : valor
6. : a commendable quality or trait : merit
7. : a capacity to act : potency
8. : chastity especially in a woman

(www.merriam-webster.com/dictionary/virtue)

I think these definitions should give us some peace of mind about self-control and virtue. Self-control is restraining yourself from doing things that will get you in trouble, to put it simply. Virtue is adhering to a moral standard, possessing strength or courage, and the willingness to use them. Do these concepts seem so foreign and unattainable now? The scriptures we're going to look at in this lesson should help clear up any lingering questions you have and will give us some ideas about how we can make these work in our lives.

Write any areas of your life in which you are struggling with self-control or virtue. What are some of the things that trip you up in this area?

Proverbs 31:1-3

The sayings of King Lemuel--an oracle his mother taught him: "O my son, O son of my womb, O son of my vows, do not spend your strength on women, your vigor on those who ruin kings." (NIV)

What does this passage tell us about Proverbs 31? Who taught these things to King Lemuel?

What kind of women do you think she is warning him about in these verses?

Why would this be something he, as a king, would need to be concerned about?

I started our reading here for this lesson because we need to remember the purpose of this proverb. This proverb is about a wife of noble character – the kind of woman King Lemuel was to look for in a wife, or possibly the woman he chose to be his wife based on things his mother had taught him. He's not to look for a flighty, bird-brained, unprincipled woman. He's to look for something more, something special.

I wanted to read this passage together to remind us as women and mothers what kind of people we should strive to be and what kind of people we want to teach our children to be. Do we want to model "loose" behavior to our children and see what happens to them in the future? How many examples have you seen that turn out badly – where bad decisions follow generation after generation without fail? We have such a huge responsibility to our children! It is up to us to equip them with the tools they need to navigate this crazy, godless world we live in, and we can't do that without equipping ourselves properly first.

Proverbs 31:10-12

A wife of noble character who can find? She is worth far more than rubies. Her husband has full confidence in her and lacks nothing of value. She brings him good, not harm, all the days of her life. (NIV)

How does this passage tie in to the concepts of self-control and virtue?

How do you think she acts?

Before you hyperventilate and start worrying about never measuring up, take a deep breath and remember what we've talked about previously. Not a single one of us on this earth is going to be this way every day. Living with a man long-term is usually enough to guarantee that there will be some slips along the way! The goal here is to strive for self-control and virtue each day, building on a firm foundation of a reverent fear of the Lord. Relying on God to help you will guarantee more success than any person can offer.

We do need to look at what this passage is saying, though. Don't you want your husband to consider you a treasure? I certainly do. If my husband has full confidence in me, I don't need to worry that he will look elsewhere for comfort or love. If I bring him good, then our home is a safe place where he can come and be strengthened and built up. If our home is not a safe place for him – if I am always critical or crabby and constantly find fault with everything he does - I am not bringing him good, am I?

Proverbs 31:28-31

Her children arise and call her blessed; her husband also, and he praises her: "Many women do noble things, but you surpass them all." Charm is deceptive, and beauty is fleeting; but a woman who fears the LORD is to be praised. Give her the reward she has earned, and let her works bring her praise at the city gate. (NIV)

What is this woman's ultimate reward from her family?

Why should we strive for this in our homes?

I know this passage talked more about fearing the Lord than self-control or virtue, but remember that we're looking at a whole person. Self-control and virtue are just two characteristics this woman illustrates for us. Again, her foundation is the fear of the Lord. Notice a common theme? She isn't someone who takes credit for her greatness; she gives the credit to God. In fact, I have a feeling she doesn't see herself as great at all – but as a woman living her life day to day loving her Lord with all her heart.

I love what the verses toward the end say, *"Her children arise and call her blessed; her husband also, and he praises her: "Many women do noble things, but you surpass them all.""* Don't you want to be that woman? We all want our children to call us blessed, don't we? We want that recognition from our husbands – how awesome those words are when spoken from the heart!

Did you know that God can help you be that woman? If you find yourself struggling with the idea of self-control or virtue, lay your burdens at His feet. Let your foundation of reverent fear and awe for God guide you as you search His word for strength and understanding. There are so many places in the Bible that can help you as you make your journey to spiritual maturity.

2 Peter 1:3-8

His divine power has given us everything we need for life and godliness through our knowledge of him who called us by his own glory and goodness. Through these he has given us his very great and precious promises, so that through them you may participate in the divine nature and escape the corruption in the world caused by evil desires. For this very reason, make every effort to add to your faith goodness; and to goodness, knowledge; and to knowledge, self-control; and to self-control, perseverance; and to perseverance, godliness; and to godliness, brotherly kindness; and to brotherly kindness, love. For if you possess these qualities in increasing measure, they will keep you from being ineffective and unproductive in your knowledge of our Lord Jesus Christ. (NIV)

What is Peter telling us in this passage?

Why do we want to strive for these qualities in our lives?

Peter is so passionate about his message, and he makes things so clear for us. He's giving us a simple list to work with. I like to think of this as a pathway to Christian maturity. Get one down, and move on to the next. As we add quality after quality we will find it easier to combat the devil and easier to live the life he wants us to. He tells us right off the bat that we already have everything available to us, thanks to the divine power of God.

Do you realize that He has set us up for success? He's already provided everything we need for life and godliness; we just have to learn about it and learn how to apply it in our lives.

Isn't God awesome? We should feel so confident after reading this passage. Knowing Christ and His heart will help us escape the corruption of this world. Of course, this means that you have to know Christ – you have to get in the word and learn. You can't trust someone else to tell you what it says. You need to open up that Bible and read it.

What is Peter's purpose in sharing the list of qualities we should strive for?

What good are we to God if we all sit around like bumps on a log? God wants us to share our knowledge with others, not keep it all to ourselves. Look at the qualities in the list again: faith, goodness, knowledge, self-control, perseverance, godliness, brotherly kindness, and love. If you want to be an effective Christian for God's kingdom, you have to be striving for these qualities. Without them you are ineffective and unproductive. What good are you to God then?

Self-control is one of the most important steps in the sequence. Without self-control the other qualities are harder, if not impossible, to obtain. How useful are you when you don't control yourself around those you're trying to evangelize? Why is your friend going to want to become a Christian when you're out there running everywhere half-cocked? Self-control is important! You have to learn to control yourself, or you run the risk of scaring others away from God forever.

1 Peter 5:6-11

Humble yourselves, therefore, under God's mighty hand, that he may lift you up in due time. Cast all your anxiety on him because he cares for you. Be self-controlled and alert. Your enemy the devil prowls around like a roaring lion looking for someone to devour. Resist him, standing firm in the faith, because you know that your brothers throughout the world are undergoing the same kind of sufferings. And the God of all grace, who called you to his eternal glory in Christ, after you have suffered a little while, will himself restore you and make you strong, firm and steadfast. To him be the power for ever and ever. Amen. (NIV)

What do you take away from this passage?

Why is self-control helpful in the situation above?

What reassurances does Peter give to those who are alert and self-controlled?

This is a passage we can take a lot of comfort from. Even though the devil is all around us looking for a good meal, we *can* resist him with Jesus' help. We are never alone in our struggles, no matter what they are. If we remember to lean on Him and His understanding and not our own, He will make us strong, firm, and steadfast. Nothing will move us. That makes me feel better about what I go through on a daily basis. Isn't it a comfort to know that He is with us through everything – big or small?

Do you ever take comfort from the fact that you're not in this alone? That's exactly what Peter is telling the Christians in this letter. We are not alone. With Him as our center, we are never on our own in this world. With other Christian sisters and brothers standing with us, we can grow and become stronger. Isn't it amazing that He has given us other Christians to help us along our journey? We can stand firm – we can control our selfish impulses – because we know that we are not in this fight alone. Other Christians are right there with us, fighting the battle at our side.

Do you find this passage comforting? Can this passage help you with the areas you are struggling with in your life? If so, how? If not, why not?

Philippians 4:4-8

Rejoice in the Lord always. I will say it again: Rejoice! Let your gentleness be evident to all. The Lord is near. Do not be anxious about anything, but in everything, by prayer and petition, with thanksgiving, present your requests to God. And the peace of God, which transcends all understanding, will guard your hearts and your minds in Christ Jesus. Finally, brothers, whatever is true, whatever is noble, whatever is right, whatever is pure, whatever is lovely, whatever is admirable--if anything is excellent or praiseworthy--think about such things. Whatever you have learned or received or heard from me, or seen in me--put it into practice. And the God of peace will be with you. (NIV)

What does this passage teach you about virtue and self-control?

What should we be focusing our minds on and why?

How can this passage help you become more self-controlled and virtuous?

What a perfect way to end this chapter! Paul has given us the formula for obtaining self-control and virtue in the span of 5 short verses. Where does our ability to control ourselves and act morally come from? Jesus, and our reliance on Him for all things. If Jesus is at the center of our actions, we can't lose. If we are faithful to present our problems and struggles to Him, He will provide. I don't know about you, but I love having the peace of God. I will take His peace over man's flawed understanding any day!

Take a look at verse 7 again, *"And the peace of God, which transcends all understanding, will guard your hearts and your minds in Christ Jesus."* God's peace will guard our hearts and minds in Christ Jesus. Doesn't that paint a beautiful picture? We have our own knight in shining armor living right in our hearts every day. If we will just cede control to Him, He will gladly guard our thoughts and actions from the world around us.

Concluding Remarks

Self-control and virtue are attainable for each one of us and should be something we want to have. God will give each one of us peace if we will just cast our cares on him. Think about areas in your life that can change when you actively practice self-control and virtue in your life as a woman, wife, and mother.

Our Proverbs 31 Woman definitely showcased these characteristics beautifully in her life and left us a good example to follow. God has shown us it's not impossible to do if we will just lean on Him. So, the decision lies with you – are you going to lean on him and let him help you be a virtuous and self-controlled woman?

Challenge

Examine the areas you are currently struggling with self-control in your life. **What is one thing you can change right now that will help you allow God to regain control of that situation? What are you doing right now that is keeping God from having control?**

Chapter 3
A Responsible Woman

Objective: To learn what it means to be a responsible woman and how to accomplish it in our lives. Learn what the Bible teaches about responsibility and meeting obligations. Look at the responsibilities we each have in our lives and how we can meet them without going crazy. Discuss the differences between physical responsibilities and spiritual responsibilities.

Responsibility

I must say this is a word my children hear quite often. The older they get, the more responsibility my husband and I try to give them. I can't tell you how many times I've reminded my older daughters, especially, of their responsibilities: writing down homework assignments, bringing homework home, turning in projects on time, picking up their rooms, and so on. Sometimes it's a never-ending mantra I repeat over and over. As their mother it is my responsibility to teach them these things and help them learn to get better at them.

I am also responsible for their spiritual guidance which is so much more daunting than any physical responsibilities I might have. It is my job as their mother to give them a firm foundation to build their own faith on, and it's a responsibility I take seriously.

As a woman, wife, and mother there are so many things I am responsible for: making a home, raising my children properly, being a loving wife, being a supportive friend, and the list goes on. Looking at the Proverbs 31 Woman's list of responsibilities, especially when compared to my own, gives me a bit of a headache.

How does she do it and maintain her sanity? The answer stems back to Lesson 1 when we talked about the fear of the Lord. Remember when I said this would be an important concept in later lessons? This is why. *Because* she was a woman who feared the Lord, he gave her the abilities to meet her responsibilities and thrive.

Does this mean we're going to read the proverb through and make ourselves to-do lists? I don't think so. We need to look at her life and how she lived it and find a pattern within it to fit ourselves.

We also need to remember that our responsibilities are not solely physical in nature. We each have spiritual responsibilities that are just as important, if not more important, than the physical things we are responsible for each day. If we are not meeting our spiritual responsibilities, we are going to find it extremely difficult to meet our physical responsibilities in a calm, capable manner.

Definitions

According to Merriam-Webster online **responsible** is defined as:

1) *a*: liable to be called on to answer

   b (1) : liable to be called to account as the primary cause, motive, or agent <a committee *responsible* for the job>

   (2) : being the cause or explanation <mechanical defects were *responsible* for the accident>

   c : liable to legal review or in case of fault to penalties

2) *a* : able to answer for one's conduct and obligations : trustworthy

   b : able to choose for oneself between right and wrong

3) : marked by or involving responsibility or accountability <*responsible* financial policies>

4) : politically answerable; *especially* : required to submit to the electorate if defeated by the legislature —used especially of the British cabinet

(www.merriam-webster.com/dictionary/responsible)

There are many directions we can go with a study about responsibility based on these definitions. If you look in the Bible, there are 44 references to the word "responsible" in the NIV. Most of them pertain to specific jobs given to people to do. In the book of Numbers alone, there are 14 references to the word! We are going to be focusing more on concept rather than word in this lesson, meaning that we're going to explore the concept of being responsible and create a picture of what a responsible woman looks like based on what we read in Scripture.

First, I want you to list out your responsibilities. What things are you responsible for on a day-to-day basis? Try to include your physical *and* spiritual responsibilities if possible.

Proverbs 31:8-9

"Speak up for those who cannot speak for themselves, for the rights of all who are destitute. Speak up and judge fairly; defend the rights of the poor and needy." (NIV)

This is the end of the section of instruction from King Lemuel's mother. What responsibilities is she pointing out to him in this passage?

Why is this important to us today?

I think this passage is important for us to look at because these are things we should all be doing as children of God. This passage isn't just for kings or those in places of power – it's for all people who profess to be Christians. We have a responsibility to others to treat them kindly and fairly, especially when they are having difficulties in life. Conversely, we should be able to rely on other Christians for help and spiritual guidance during our own times of struggle.

There are so many ways we can express this passage in our lives. Obviously, we can help the poor and needy in many ways – charities, volunteering, counseling, and donating items to name a few. But do you ever think about what you can do for the spiritually needy people that you come across every day? If you volunteer with a shelter, you certainly run into plenty of people who need spiritual food just as much as they need physical food.

What can you do to meet this need in the people around you?

Proverbs 31:15-22

She gets up while it is still dark; she provides food for her family and portions for her servant girls. She considers a field and buys it; out of her earnings she plants a vineyard. She sets about her work vigorously; her arms are strong for her tasks. She sees that her trading is profitable, and her lamp does not go out at night. In her hand she holds the distaff and grasps the spindle with her fingers. She opens her arms to the poor and extends her hands to the needy. When it snows, she has no fear for her household; for all of them are clothed in scarlet. She makes coverings for her bed; she is clothed in fine linen and purple. (NIV)

What are some of the things the Proverbs 31 Woman is responsible for?

How does her list of responsibilities compare to yours?

How does her list make you feel comparatively?

What stands out most to you in this list? Why?

This is one of the passages of Proverbs 31 that gives us the most trouble. We read this and immediately think we can never live up to this woman's example. There's no way I can follow her schedule every day and stay sane. We allow her schedule to intimidate us instead of reading this and figuring out how to implement some of her techniques into our lives.

What do I mean?

Let's break down some of the responsibilities she has:

- She takes care of her household;
- She budgets and spends her money wisely;
- She works hard;
- She's generous and kind;
- She's organized and well-prepared.

I don't know about you, but that is a list I can get behind! These are all qualities that I want to strive for in my life and better yet, they are all qualities I can learn about in the Bible. Isn't it amazing how God gives us examples of women we can look up to?

Take a moment and look at her list again. Think about what things on that list give you the most trouble in your life.

List them here:

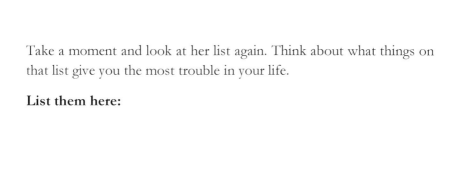

I want you to particularly focus on these items while you go through this chapter. Use the passages we're studying to encourage you and help you accomplish your goal. If you need to write verses down and post them around the house, feel free to do so. Sometimes we need that visual reminder when we're trying to make changes.

Ruth 1:15-18

"Look," said Naomi, "your sister-in-law is going back to her people and her gods. Go back with her." But Ruth replied, "Don't urge me to leave you or to turn back from you. Where you go I will go, and where you stay I will stay. Your people will be my people and your God my God. Where you die I will die, and there I will be buried. May the LORD deal with me, be it ever so severely, if anything but death separates you and me." When Naomi realized that Ruth was determined to go with her, she stopped urging her. (NIV)

Why do you think Ruth was willing to travel to a foreign country, as a widow, with her mother-in-law?

Is this a responsibility she was expected to take on?

What is she willingly leaving behind in Moab?

Put yourself in Ruth's place. What would you have done? Why?

Ruth is, to me, the epitome of a responsible woman, and I love reading her story in the Bible. It's got a gutsy heroine who makes huge sacrifices for her mother-in-law, endures struggles and difficulties with grace, and finds love and happiness in the end. She was obviously a woman who was not afraid of taking on responsibility in many forms. I admire her passion and drive, and it makes me wonder if I would do the same thing in her position.

We all like to think we would be this way, right? Willing to give up everything we know, love, and care about to care for our husband's mother? But would you? Would you leave your family, your friends, your world forever?

Spiritually, Ruth was leaving behind the gods of Moab to take God as her own. Much like people who choose to convert from different religions to Christianity today, this was another huge burden and responsibility for her. Even more than the distance that would separate them physically, she made a choice that would forever separate her from her family spiritually. She clearly states to Naomi that God will be her God from now on. There is no half-way with this woman. She is all-in for the long haul, both physically and spiritually. She's leaving behind not only her family, but her culture, religion, friends, and everything she knows in order to take responsibility for her mother-in-law.

I think Ruth and our Proverbs 31 Woman would get along quite well. If you read through the book of Ruth, you learn that her decision in this passage works out well for her. So well, in fact, that she is King David's great-grandmother! She is one of the few women mentioned in Jesus' genealogy by name. She receives many rewards for her selfless behavior both in her lifetime and in her descendants' lives after her. I hope I bless my family with the decisions I make in my life – don't you?

Esther 4:6-17

So Hathach went out to Mordecai in the open square of the city in front of the king's gate. Mordecai told him everything that had happened to him, including the exact amount of money Haman had promised to pay into the royal treasury for the destruction of the Jews. He also gave him a copy of the text of the edict for their annihilation, which had been published in Susa, to show to Esther and explain it to her, and he told him to urge her to go into the king's presence to beg for mercy and plead with him for her people. Hathach went back and reported to Esther what Mordecai had said. Then she instructed him to say to Mordecai, "All the king's officials and the people of the royal provinces know that for any man or woman who approaches the king in the inner court without being summoned the king has but one law: that he be put to death. The only exception to this is for the king to extend the gold scepter to him and spare his life. But thirty days have passed since I was called to go to the king." When Esther's words were reported to Mordecai, he sent back this answer: "Do not think that because you are in the king's house you alone of all the Jews will escape. For if you remain silent at this time, relief and deliverance for the Jews will arise from another place, but you and your father's family will perish. And who knows but that you have come to royal position for such a time as this?" Then Esther sent this reply to Mordecai: "Go, gather together all the Jews who are in Susa, and fast for me. Do not eat or drink for three days, night or day. I and my maids will fast as you do. When this is done, I will go to the king, even though it is against the law. And if I perish, I perish." So Mordecai went away and carried out all of Esther's instructions. (NIV)

Tell me a little bit about Esther's responsibilities in this passage.

Can you identify with her position at all?

Do you think we are put in situations like this today? Why or why not?

Esther is another awesome Bible woman who has a neat story. If you don't know it, I would encourage you to go read it – it's only 10 chapters, and it's full of action, romance, and adventure. From the passage we just read, you can see that the Jews were facing extermination due to machinations by a man named Haman. Esther, as queen, was the Jews' only hope at salvation. But she had to approach her husband, King Xerxes, without being summoned, which could get her killed if he wished it.

I will spoil it and tell you that he was actually pleased to see her, and because of her bravery and willingness to take responsibility for her people on her shoulders, she helps save the Jews.

She had quite the responsibility, didn't she? I can't imagine being in her position – I hope I would be so brave. What are some things we deal with that might compare with her situation? The day may come in our country when we aren't supposed to assemble and worship as Christians. We would have a hard decision to make at that time, wouldn't we? Do we follow God even at risk of our own lives?

As Christians we have a responsibility to stand up for the gospel at all costs. Are God and His message that important to you? If not, this might be a good time to think about why that is and how you might change that today.

Ephesians 4:1-16

As a prisoner for the Lord, then, I urge you to live a life worthy of the calling you have received. Be completely humble and gentle; be patient, bearing with one another in love. Make every effort to keep the unity of the Spirit through the bond of peace. There is one body and one Spirit--just as you were called to one hope when you were called-- one Lord, one faith, one baptism; one God and Father of all, who is over all and through all and in all. But to each one of us grace has been given as Christ apportioned it. This is why it says: "When he ascended on high, he led captives in his train and gave gifts to men." (What does "he ascended" mean except that he also descended to the lower, earthly regions? He who descended is the very one who ascended higher than all the heavens, in order to fill the whole universe.) It was he who gave some to be apostles, some to be prophets, some to be evangelists, and some to be pastors and teachers, to prepare God's people for works of service, so that the body of Christ may be built up until we all reach unity in the faith and in the knowledge of the Son of God and become mature, attaining to the whole measure of the fullness of Christ. Then we will no longer be infants, tossed back and forth by the waves, and blown here and there by every wind of teaching and by the cunning and craftiness of men in their deceitful scheming. Instead, speaking the truth in love, we will in all things grow up into him who is the Head, that is, Christ. From him the whole body, joined and held together by every supporting ligament, grows and builds itself up in love, as each part does its work. (NIV)

What does this passage teach you about responsibilities?

What work has God given us to do?

What responsibilities has God given you?

After reading about such great examples of responsible, Godly women we needed a passage that helps us learn how to get it for ourselves. Paul is a wonderful teacher and all of his letters are full of ways we can grow and learn in our Christian walk. So, what do we learn from this passage? We see a picture of spiritual growth that we can all work toward.

Do you want to be stronger? Do you wonder whether God has any plans for you? Are you curious about your gifts and abilities? This passage delves into all those things for you. We learn that to be strong we need to be patient, kind, gentle, unified, and firm in our faith in Christ. We learn that God has plans for each one of us, and when we find our spiritual place we find ultimate fulfillment in our work.

This is another passage we need to keep ready in our minds. I don't know how many people I have run into who are unsure about their purpose. They wonder what God has planned for them, they wonder why He doesn't work on their timetable, and they really want to know RIGHT NOW what their spiritual gift is so they can share it with everyone. Sound familiar? At some point we all go through this. The key is not to get stuck in this place – let God teach you what He wants from you. Read your Bible so you can learn more about Him. Participate in Bible studies with fellow Christians so you can learn even more. Pray constantly so that you can become the Christian God needs you to be. Your gifts will become clear the more you work in His kingdom.

Philippians 3:12-21

Not that I have already obtained all this, or have already been made perfect, but I press on to take hold of that for which Christ Jesus took hold of me. Brothers, I do not consider myself yet to have taken hold of it. But one thing I do: Forgetting what is behind and straining toward what is ahead, I press on toward the goal to win the prize for which God has called me heavenward in Christ Jesus. All of us who are mature should take such a view of things. And if on some point you think differently, that too God will make clear to you. Only let us live up to what we have already attained. Join with others in following my example, brothers, and take note of those who live according to the pattern we gave you. For, as I have often told you before and now say again even with tears, many live as enemies of the cross of Christ. Their destiny is destruction, their god is their stomach, and their glory is in their shame. Their mind is on earthly things. But our citizenship is in heaven. And we eagerly await a Savior from there, the Lord Jesus Christ, who, by the power that enables him to bring everything under his control, will transform our lowly bodies so that they will be like his glorious body. (NIV)

What does this passage say to you?

What is our reward for being responsible Christians?

What do you learn about responsibility from these verses?

This passage doesn't spell out our responsibilities as Christians, but it does paint a good picture of our goal here. We are pressing forward, looking ahead to the goal set our before us – eternity with our Lord and Savior Jesus Christ. What is our responsibility? Live in such a way that we win our prize. Our minds should be on that prize every day, and our lives should reflect our citizenship in Heaven.

Paul also reminds us that we have to remember those who haven't chosen Christ. Does it ever bother you to think about all the lost souls walking the street with you? It can get overwhelming if we let it. What do we do? I think Paul answers that question for us, too – we press on and show them what it means to be a Christian. I know I have loved ones in my life who have chosen to reject God and I hope that someday I will be able to help steer them back to Him. I pray for them every day and work hard to be a good example of a Christian to them.

Meanwhile, I am working on myself and striving to become stronger in my faith and knowledge every day so that I will be ready. I love how Paul mentions looking forward, not back. We all need that reminder – we can't change the things that have passed, only those that lay ahead. We will also miss out on the things God has planned for us if we insist on living in our past mistakes. We have to learn to look ahead:
"Forgetting what is behind and straining toward what is ahead, I press on toward the goal to win the prize for which God has called me heavenward in Christ Jesus."

Don't forget the prize you are striving toward. Eternity with God in heaven is waiting. Don't let it go!

Concluding Remarks

Look back at the list of responsibilities you wrote at the beginning of the lesson.

Are there things on that list that weigh you down, frustrate you, or that feel unattainable?

How many things are on your list that don't need to be there?

Have you taken on some things more out of a sense of guilt than a true eagerness or interest?

Are you trying to do things to make others happy or fill gaps left by others who don't hold up their end?

Are you busy being Super-Mom the Activity Shuffler and too busy to talk to your kids about spiritual matters and responsibilities?

Spend some time with your list in prayer. If you have taken on responsibilities that are causing a struggle for you, take it to God in prayer. He will take your burdens on his shoulders. Learn from our Proverbs 31 Woman, Ruth, and Esther – don't let your responsibilities get in between you and your Creator.

"Cast your cares on the LORD and he will sustain you; he will never let the righteous fall." (Psalm 55:22, NIV)

He is here for you: to help you meet responsibilities you need to meet; to help you with the responsibility of raising your children in a Godly manner; to make the hard decisions when you're in over your head. Let him help. Your life will never be the same afterwards!

Challenge

Think about the list of responsibilities you made at the beginning of this lesson. **What things on your list are most important? Which ones can go? How will your life change as you get your responsibilities in order?**

Chapter 4
A Kind and Compassionate Woman

Objective: Learn what it means to be a kind and compassionate Christian woman. Learn how to improve our ability to act with kindness and compassion to others in all situations we find ourselves in. Learn why these are important characteristics to have.

Kindness and Compassion

I think these are two words we as women hear a lot, both as girls growing up and ladies making our way through the world. A lady is to be kind and compassionate at all times to all people without fail, right? What images do these terms bring to mind for you? Is there a particular person you know who personifies these characteristics? How do you do with being kind and compassionate to others… to yourself?

Our Proverbs 31 Woman was a kind and compassionate woman, as we read in the proverb. She not only cared for her husband and family but also for her servant girls and the needy in her community. She was able to do this because of her close relationship with the Lord. Again, I'm back to that fear of the Lord phrase that we know and love so well by this point. She lets her trust and reliance on the Lord guide everything she does in her life. Does that mean that she never speaks a cross word or hurts someone's feelings? Probably not, since she is a woman with children and a husband as well as responsibilities in her community. But we know that her overall attitude toward others is one of kindness and compassion given to her by God.

Are these concepts that come naturally to you or do you have to work for them? We are all different, so I expect some of you are dreading this lesson while others are waiting with baited breath. If you aren't naturally kind and compassionate, don't worry. We're going to work on that together as you progress through this. Fortunately for you, God has provided everything you need in His word.

Definitions

Kind (as an adjective) is defined as:

1. chiefly dialect **:** <u>affectionate</u>, <u>loving</u>
2. a **:** of a sympathetic or helpful nature
   b **:** of a forbearing nature **:** <u>gentle</u>
   c **:** arising from or characterized by sympathy or forbearance
   <a kind act>
1. **:** of a kind to give pleasure or relief

(<u>www.merriam-webster.com/dictionary/kind</u>)

Compassion is defined as:

1. **:** sympathetic <u>consciousness</u> of others' distress together with a desire to alleviate it

(<u>www.merriam-webster.com/compassion</u>)

What these definitions say to me is that kindness and compassion are all about attitude – making a conscious choice in behavior. Notice that parts 2)a and 2)b of kind's definition talk about nature, what comes naturally to you. Obviously this means that it will be easier for some people to exhibit this characteristic than others. Compassion is all about being conscious of another's distress and actually caring about it. I think we can agree that some people naturally exhibit these characteristics, and others have to work hard to exhibit them.

Now, before you get excited and think you're off the hook because you have a different nature, think again. God expects all of his children to exhibit these characteristics as Christ did. If you have to work to be kind and compassionate, they will be qualities you value more for the work you have to do to get them.

Proverbs 31:15; 20-21

She gets up while it is still dark; she provides food for her family and portions for her servant girls. (NIV)

She opens her arms to the poor and extends her hands to the needy. When it snows, she has no fear for her household; for all of them are clothed in scarlet. (NIV)

What mental images do these verses bring to your mind?

What emotional reaction, if any, do you have to these verses?

What can you infer about her relationship with her family from these verses?

What can you infer about her relationship/position in the community at large from these verses?

What kind of woman is she to those outside her immediate family and household?

These verses create a picture of a kind and compassionate woman and how she interacts with her family, household, and strangers. I see it as a bit of a snapshot into the Proverbs 31 Woman's life. You might notice that none of the activities in the verses above are anything elaborate or particularly difficult to do. She is simply choosing to live her life a certain way, and others are benefitting from that choice.

Is this someone slinging breakfast dishes across the table, huffing under her breath about how early she started her day to put this food on the table? Can you see her banging pots around while she's cooking so everyone knows she's going to the trouble of making them breakfast? Obviously not. It seems like she gets up early and performs this service for her household because she wants to. There is no ulterior motive or martyr's attitude about it. She's doing it out of love which is exhibiting itself in kindness to her family and household.

I think we can see from verses 20 – 21 that she lovingly opens her arms to those who need her. It creates a beautiful picture in my head. I see a woman who genuinely loves people and cares for their well-being. Clothing her household in scarlet signifies that her people are well provided for and comfortable for the winter. Providing scarlet clothing means that it was dyed, not a cheap process, and certainly not something that most people provided for their servants during any period in history.

Are these things you think you can emulate in your life? I'm sure you can think of ways to serve your family and community that will make a positive difference. God blesses us and throws many opportunities our way every day – sometimes they're as simple as helping the children with homework or making your husband's favorite dish for dinner, other times you might find yourself in a position to serve in a shelter or hold Bible studies at your church. What we need to learn from our Proverbs 31 Woman is to be ready when those opportunities arise. God will send people into our lives and give us chances to bless every day – we have to be in sync with Him so we are ready to serve.

Luke 6:27-36

"But I tell you who hear me: Love your enemies, do good to those who hate you, bless those who curse you, pray for those who mistreat you. If someone strikes you on one cheek, turn to him the other also. If someone takes your cloak, do not stop him from taking your tunic. Give to everyone who asks you, and if anyone takes what belongs to you, do not demand it back. Do to others as you would have them do to you. "If you love those who love you, what credit is that to you? Even 'sinners' love those who love them. And if you do good to those who are good to you, what credit is that to you? Even 'sinners' do that. And if you lend to those from whom you expect repayment, what credit is that to you? Even 'sinners' lend to 'sinners,' expecting to be repaid in full. But love your enemies, do good to them, and lend to them without expecting to get anything back. Then your reward will be great, and you will be sons of the Most High, because he is kind to the ungrateful and wicked. Be merciful, just as your Father is merciful. (NIV)

What does this passage say to you?

How are we to behave toward people who treat us badly? Why?

How can you put this principle into practice in your life?

Ouch! This is a passage that none of us likes to look at too closely. Who wants to love their enemy and be nice to people who hate them and curse them? That's too hard! I have to say this is a passage I have struggled with in my life over the last few years. It is difficult to be kind to someone who is determined to do you harm. Our culture makes it even harder because it says not to be doormats, to stand up for ourselves, and to get them before they get us. All of these competing ideas combine to make for some confused Christian women in times of conflict. Let's look at what this passage is saying and see if we can gain some clarity.

The first part of the passage is all about how we interact with others, especially those whom we are having trouble with. It ends with the golden rule, *"Do to others as you would have them do to you."* We like to use this verse as an excuse for returning tit for tat when we're involved in a conflict. It's easy to look at this verse and turn it on whomever you're fighting with. Not so easy to look at it as it applies to you directly.

We are the ones who are to do to others as we'd have done to us, no matter how others treat us at the moment. In all things we are to emulate Christ and his behavior. He loved his enemies to the point of praying for them on the cross they hung him on. Don't you think we can work on not getting quite so hot under the collar when someone hurts us?

The second part of the passage is the wake-up call for us. To sum it up, we don't get to take the easy way out when we choose to be a Christian. Those who live in the world do the easy stuff all the time, so God expects us to do more. We *have* to do more if we want to show Jesus to others who need it. Think of how we will stand out if we do the unexpected – show kindness when none is warranted.

2 Timothy 2:22-26

Flee the evil desires of youth, and pursue righteousness, faith, love and peace, along with those who call on the Lord out of a pure heart. Don't have anything to do with foolish and stupid arguments, because you know they produce quarrels. And the Lord's servant must not quarrel; instead, he must be kind to everyone, able to teach, not resentful. Those who oppose him he must gently instruct, in the hope that God will grant them repentance leading them to a knowledge of the truth, and that they will come to their senses and escape from the trap of the devil, who has taken them captive to do his will. (NIV)

Describe the attitude we are to have based on this passage.

How are we to interact with those who oppose us and why?

Why do you think Paul stresses that we are to be kind to everyone?

This is a straightforward passage, and I love how Paul words things. It makes it clear to me that being kind is a choice we all have to make, especially when it's difficult. One thing Paul points out that we need to look at is why we should be gentle with those who cause us problems. Our hope should be to bring them to repentance and a relationship with Christ, saving them from the devil's trap.

How often do we think of this during the heat of battle? Do we really care about the hold the devil has on whomever we're fighting with, or are we so focused on being right and vindicated that we set it aside? Do we invite the devil into our hearts when we do this?

We have to remember that we are not to be resentful toward those who oppose us. Easy words, but what a difficult concept. I think one reason Paul stresses this so much is that feelings of resentment and anger open us up to Satan's machinations. Remember from earlier lessons, the devil is prowling around like a lion waiting to devour us. What good are we going to be to the kingdom if we fall right into the devil's trap by holding on to hard feelings?

Think for a moment of the impact we could have on our culture if we fully embraced the ideas presented in this passage. Our churches would certainly look different, wouldn't they? Sometimes I think we Christians love to hold on to our foolish arguments and quarrels while we ignore all the people hurting around us, still caught in Satan's grasp. How much time do we waste arguing amongst ourselves while the enemy goes about growing in strength because we're useless? We have to be compassionate with one another. Does this mean we never disagree? Of course not – it means that when we disagree we take positive measures to come to a resolution and leave the hard feelings and anger out of it. What a difference we could make by simply implementing this principle in our lives.

Colossians 3:13-17

Therefore, as God's chosen people, holy and dearly loved, clothe yourselves with compassion, kindness, humility, gentleness and patience. Bear with each other and forgive whatever grievances you may have against one another. Forgive as the Lord forgave you. And over all these virtues put on love, which binds them all together in perfect unity. Let the peace of Christ rule in your hearts, since as members of one body you were called to peace. And be thankful. Let the word of Christ dwell in you richly as you teach and admonish one another with all wisdom, and as you sing psalms, hymns and spiritual songs with gratitude in your hearts to God. And whatever you do, whether in word or deed, do it all in the name of the Lord Jesus, giving thanks to God the Father through him. (NIV)

What does this passage mean to you?

What kind of relationships are we to have with other believers?

How are we to behave when a Christian sister wrongs us?

I love the imagery of clothing in this passage. I like to think of putting on my compassion, kindness, humility, gentleness, and patience every day before I leave the house. Over all these things I should wear love because it brings the outfit together and creates a whole Christian. It's also easy to visualize what is likely to happen if I forget my compassion or *insert virtue here* at home.

Again, God calls on us to forgive grievances. In this case, these are grievances we have with someone in the body of Christ. In my experience, this is usually more difficult to do with fellow Christians than it is with those outside the church.

Why is that? Why do we have such a hard time forgiving a Christian sister or brother who has wronged us?

Look back at the passage again. *"Forgive as the Lord forgave you."* This is such a short sentence and so easy to overlook in the passage as a whole, but it's quite a whopper! What right do I have to hold a grudge against my brother when God doesn't hold a grudge against me, sinner that I am? It puts things into perspective, doesn't it? We're to put love over all the other virtues listed which will bind us all together. Pure, Christ-like love can overcome any issue we have with each other.

There are so many lessons for us in this short passage of scripture. We can see why kindness and compassion are important characteristics for us to have and use, especially toward Christian brothers and sisters. We are to do everything in the name of Jesus Christ which should guide our day-to-day lives. With Christ as our guide, we can navigate this world with our Christian clothes secure and fully functional.

Titus 3:3-8

At one time we too were foolish, disobedient, deceived and enslaved by all kinds of passions and pleasures. We lived in malice and envy, being hated and hating one another. But when the kindness and love of God our Savior appeared, he saved us, not because of righteous things we had done, but because of his mercy. He saved us through the washing of rebirth and renewal by the Holy Spirit, whom he poured out on us generously through Jesus Christ our Savior, so that, having been justified by his grace, we might become heirs having the hope of eternal life. This is a trustworthy saying. And I want you to stress these things, so that those who have trusted in God may be careful to devote themselves to doing what is good. These things are excellent and profitable for everyone. (NIV)

What is the message of this passage?

Why is important to our lesson?

How does this passage affect you and your life?

What a wake-up call to Christians! I think we catch ourselves in the trap of "us -Christians" vs. "them - Sinners" and forget that we are all sinners in need of Christ's mercy and grace. We forget that before we were Christians, we were guilty of all the sins listed in these verses. No one but Christ has ever lived on this earth without sinning, and without him we would be condemned forever. Because of his kindness and mercy to us, we have the opportunity to change our lives, live for him, and spend eternity with him someday. If we spend more time showing kindness to others and doing what is good, we will have such a huge impact on our world.

I find it interesting that Paul specifically tells Titus to stress "these things" with the church there in Crete. In other words, the church there needed a reminder that they were not perfect and that they were no better than the unsaved masses around them. Does this sound familiar? I think that our churches could often benefit from such a letter. We are so quick to forget that we are all sinners saved by the blood of Jesus Christ and scooped from the path to destruction by His mercy. We're not examples of perfection floating on clouds above the rest of the world. We should be shining examples of grace and mercy – ready to share with everyone we come across the wonderful things God has done for us.

What can we learn about kindness and compassion from this passage? Quite a bit, I think. For instance, we learn that we should have compassion on our newer brothers and sisters who are just coming to know Jesus, especially since they are where we were at one time. We also learn some humility from these verses. Any time you start thinking you're hot stuff in the Christian department and compare yourself to those around you, I challenge you to re-read this passage. It never hurts to remember where you have come from. We should be proud of the accomplishments we have made for the kingdom, but we need to remember that it is God who allows us to accomplish those things – not our personal greatness.

Ephesians 4:29-32

Do not let any unwholesome talk come out of your mouths, but only what is helpful for building others up according to their needs, that it may benefit those who listen. And do not grieve the Holy Spirit of God, with whom you were sealed for the day of redemption. Get rid of all bitterness, rage and anger, brawling and slander, along with every form of malice. Be kind and compassionate to one another, forgiving each other, just as in Christ God forgave you. (NIV)

What instructions does Paul give us in this passage?

How can your life change if you implement the behaviors discussed here?

Does this mean that we can't correct or point out a sin in a brother or sister? Why or why not?

This is a powerful passage to me. Paul doesn't mince words, as usual, and we can grow enormously if we absorb the message here. What is he saying to us? We need to empty out the garbage inside of us, and let the spirit of Christ fill us. We need to put others before ourselves, and think before we speak. We need to genuinely care for one another as Christ cares for us. It's a fairly simple list, but boy is it full of tough things for us to handle! It's so easy to say we're going to be compassionate and kind, but it's not so easy to put into practice.

The relationship between kindness, compassion, and forgiveness makes itself apparent once again in these verses. Have you ever thought about the relationship between these three things? It makes perfect sense if you think about it. Without kindness or compassion, you can't forgive. Forgiveness requires you to step outside of yourself and think about someone else. You can't do that without compassion. Every time you choose compassion over judgment or anger you work for the kingdom. Isn't that amazing?

I think it's also important to point out how important watching your words is to God. How many times have you seen a situation spiral out of control because someone doesn't censor their words? Think one moment about the impact you can have on those around you if you make a concentrated effort to only speak encouraging, uplifting words.

Does this mean you'll never have disagreements? Unfortunately no, but if you are letting God work through you He can help during difficult situations. Look at the things we're supposed to eliminate: bitterness, rage and anger, brawling and slander, and every form of malice. Without these in your heart you'll find forgiveness, kindness, and compassion much easier to obtain.

Concluding Remarks

I think we will notice positive changes in our lives, as well as our churches, if we can learn to be kind and compassionate women. It's not an impossible task for any of us, and none of us are going to do it perfectly. But imagine for a moment what your life would be like if you could put resentments and petty differences aside and focus instead on being kind, compassionate, and loving toward those you interact with each day.

How are you going to work on being a more kind and compassionate person?

What do you think your biggest challenge will be?

Take your challenges to the Lord in prayer. He is the only one who can give you the strength to change your behaviors. Share your struggles and successes with your Christian sisters, and gain strength from them. Your life will be so much better in so many ways.

Challenge

Write down one person you have a difficult time being kind and compassionate to. **Your challenge is to lift this person up in prayer every day for at least one week – pray FOR them, not ABOUT them – and ask God to help you show them kindness and compassion. Write your successes and failures below.**

Chapter 5
A Hardworking and Resourceful Woman

Objective: Learn what it means to be a hardworking and resourceful Christian woman and how it looks different for each one of us. Learn how we become hardworking, resourceful women in God's kingdom. Identify the pitfalls we run into, and learn how we can overcome them.

Hardworking and Resourceful

Any time I see or hear the word resourceful I think of MacGyver, the 80's TV show with Richard Dean Anderson. He was an agent for a secret government agency who could do just about anything with duct tape and his pocket knife. No matter what tough situation he found himself in, he came up with a creative, resourceful way to get out of it and saved the day while he was at it.

Some of the hardest workers I have ever known are the farmers and ranchers I grew up around. From dawn to dark, especially during harvest time, they are out working in the fields or with the animals. It is exhausting, back-breaking work, but they are some of the most satisfied and happy people I have ever come across.

Our Proverbs 31 Woman knew all about being hardworking and resourceful. There are so many examples in the proverb of things she accomplished, it can make your head hurt! She was a landowner, wool spinner, philanthropist, seamstress, wife, and mother, among other things.

How do we plan to live up to that image? Are we going to formulate business plans and conduct sewing demonstrations during this Bible study? No, but we are going to examine the heart and attitude behind all of her ventures. Again, by relying on God for her strength and vigor, she was able to accomplish much with her life. We have that same ability at our fingertips if we choose to reach out and take it.

Definitions

Hardworking is defined as:

: <u>industrious</u>, <u>diligent</u>

(<u>www.merriam-webster.com/dictionary/hardworking</u>)

Resourceful is defined as:

: able to meet situations : capable of devising ways and means <a
resourceful leader>

(<u>www.merriam-webster.com/resourceful</u>)

These are straightforward definitions for straightforward terms. I
think we're all comfortable with what it means to be hardworking and
resourceful. Our challenge is applying this to our spiritual walk and
seeing what the Bible has to say about these concepts.

Proverbs 31:13-19; 21-24; 27

She selects wool and flax and works with eager hands. She is like the merchant ships, bringing her food from afar. She gets up while it is still dark; she provides food for her family and portions for her servant girls. She considers a field and buys it; out of her earnings she plants a vineyard. She sets about her work vigorously; her arms are strong for her tasks. She sees that her trading is profitable, and her lamp does not go out at night. In her hand she holds the distaff and grasps the spindle with her fingers. (NIV)

When it snows, she has no fear for her household; for all of them are clothed in scarlet. She makes coverings for her bed; she is clothed in fine linen and purple. Her husband is respected at the city gate, where he takes his seat among the elders of the land. She makes linen garments and sells them, and supplies the merchants with sashes. (NIV)

She watches over the affairs of her household and does not eat the bread of idleness. (NIV)

What kinds of activities does the Proverbs 31 Woman keep herself busy with?

How do you think you measure up to this woman?

It's easy to look at these verses and tell ourselves we'll never measure up to such an impossible task. But what if we break down the list, and look at what she's doing? Maybe it's not such an impossible goal after all.

1. She's a selective shopper – she likes quality and takes her time finding it.
2. She takes care of her family and entire household.
3. She makes good decisions about investments by thinking them through and researching them carefully.
4. She budgets and uses her money wisely so that her family and household can live comfortably.
5. She is an entrepreneur and business-savvy.

Looking at the list above, how many of these things are you doing right now?

Which ones, if any, do you think are impossible for you to achieve?

We often read this proverb and feel so overwhelmed by all that this woman does and accomplishes that we get frustrated and give up on ourselves. Maybe we think that because we don't own a business we can't measure up. Or that we can't sew a straight seam if our life depended on it, so we'll never be like this woman.

I have some questions for you if you're feeling inadequate after reading the list above: How many of us did God make exactly the same? Do we live in a world of carbon copies? How effective are we going to be as a society if we all do the exact same thing? We can take the principles listed above and apply them to our lives, but our lists will never end up the same. I think there are pieces of everything on the list that we can aspire to and achieve in our lives.

Is your selective shopping going to be the same as mine? Probably not – we have different needs, wants, and interests. But we can certainly share information with each other about different stores and deals we come across, and respect the differences in what we each want and need.

Is your household going to run exactly the same as mine? Of course not. But we can work together to make sure that we're putting God first in our own lives, as well as those of our families, and we can support one another as we grow and mature as mothers and wives. We can share tips for getting hot meals on the table, keeping laundry caught up, and digging out from under that pile of ironing.

Are our budgets going to be the same? No way! There are so many factors that affect this part of our lives; we all have to work our family budgets out for ourselves. This doesn't mean that we can't share money saving tips with one another or rejoice when we get a raise or a new job.

Some of us are going to be entrepreneurs, professionals, business owners, or maybe cottage industry workers, but not all of us. Some of us are going to be housewives or homeschooling moms and work hard at that. You don't have to own a business to be smart about engaging in commerce – you just need common sense and God-given intellect. We can still respect one another as Christian women who love our families and work together for the good of the Lord.

The Parable of the Talents

"Again, it will be like a man going on a journey, who called his servants and entrusted his property to them. To one he gave five talents of money, to another two talents, and to another one talent, each according to his ability. Then he went on his journey. The man who had received the five talents went at once and put his money to work and gained five more. So also, the one with the two talents gained two more. But the man who had received the one talent went off, dug a hole in the ground and hid his master's money. "After a long time the master of those servants returned and settled accounts with them. The man who had received the five talents brought the other five. 'Master,' he said, 'you entrusted me with five talents. See, I have gained five more.' "His master replied, 'Well done, good and faithful servant! You have been faithful with a few things; I will put you in charge of many things. Come and share your master's happiness!' "The man with the two talents also came. 'Master,' he said, 'you entrusted me with two talents; see, I have gained two more.' "His master replied, 'Well done, good and faithful servant! You have been faithful with a few things; I will put you in charge of many things. Come and share your master's happiness!' "Then the man who had received the one talent came. 'Master,' he said, 'I knew that you are a hard man, harvesting where you have not sown and gathering where you have not scattered seed. So I was afraid and went out and hid your talent in the ground. See, here is what belongs to you.' "His master replied, 'You wicked, lazy servant! So you knew that I harvest where I have not sown and gather where I have not scattered seed? Well then, you should have put my money on deposit with the bankers, so that when I returned I would have received it back with interest. " 'Take the talent from him and give it to the one who has the ten talents. For everyone who has will be given more, and he will have an abundance. Whoever does not have, even what he has will be taken from him. And throw that worthless servant outside, into the darkness, where there will be weeping and gnashing of teeth.' (NIV)

What does this parable teach us about being hardworking and resourceful, if anything?

What does God expect of us?

What are some ways you can be hardworking and resourceful for the kingdom?

What are some things we do to sabotage the work of the kingdom?

This is such a neat parable to read, and yet it's sobering as well. Jesus is telling us what God expects of us, and he makes it clear to us what will happen if we choose to be lazy and ignore our job. God has blessed us all with particular talents and abilities. He expects us to use those talents and abilities to further his kingdom here on Earth.

You may notice the man (i.e. God) gave responsibilities and expectations based on what his servants could handle. He didn't hand each man 5 talents and expect them to earn 5 more. He did, however, expect the man with 1 talent to do something with it. He would have been pleased if the man had taken it to the bank and let it collect interest instead of hiding it away in the ground. The men who worked hard and showed initiative (were resourceful) were blessed, while the man who chose not to work and showed no initiative was thrown out.

Have you ever stopped to wonder what would have happened if any of the servants had invested the money and lost it? What do you think the response would have been? I happen to think that the master (God) would have been fine with the loss because the servant was doing something to try and help his master. In the same way, we can't let fear of failure hold us back. If we are earnestly working for God in His kingdom and we suffer failure, He's not going to throw us to the wolves. We can't let that fear rule us.

He wants us to work hard for Him, no matter the results. Maybe you spend months witnessing to your neighbor, only to have her completely turn away from you and the church forever. Will God punish you for this? No – if you were doing what is right and working for Him – He knows you can't control everyone around you.

If we stick ourselves out there, we're going to fail at one point or another. That's part of being a Christian. People are going to reject God, no matter how hard we try to save them. The point is we have to TRY. If we don't try to save those around us, we will certainly fail and God holds us accountable for it.

He's not asking us all to go out and be the next famous evangelist or Christian superstar, but he is asking each of us to do whatever we can with the talents we have to bring glory to His name.

Luke 10:38-42

As Jesus and his disciples were on their way, he came to a village where a woman named Martha opened her home to him. She had a sister called Mary, who sat at the Lord's feet listening to what he said. But Martha was distracted by all the preparations that had to be made. She came to him and asked, "Lord, don't you care that my sister has left me to do the work by myself? Tell her to help me!" "Martha, Martha," the Lord answered, "you are worried and upset about many things, but only one thing is needed. Mary has chosen what is better, and it will not be taken away from her." (NIV)

Who do you identify with more in this story? Why?

If you were Martha, how do you think you would you have reacted in the situation?

I will be honest and say that I would be more like Martha in this story, except I wouldn't have complained out loud. I might have slammed a few cabinets, or whatever the Biblical equivalent would be, but I wouldn't have *said* anything to Jesus or Mary. I can only imagine the stress of preparing for guests, coupled with the fact that it was JESUS in her house, made Martha a nervous wreck. Understandably so, don't you think?

But look at how Jesus speaks to her. He pretty much tells her to stop sweating the small stuff, and focus on what's important: the message of Jesus. Wow! That'll stop you in your tracks, won't it? Does this mean that it's OK to serve baloney sandwiches on a Sunday afternoon if it means you're sharing God's word with someone? Surely it can't mean that I can host a Bible study if my house isn't perfect?!

Those of us like Martha can actually draw a lot of comfort from this passage if we stop and realize that Jesus' priorities are not always the same as ours. While he wants us to be loving and kind hostesses, we shouldn't concentrate on the physical work (meal prep, housecleaning, etc.) to the exclusion of his Master plan – saving the lost and sharing the message of the Gospel.

The kingdom is not going to suffer if my house is not perfect when I share the gospel message with a neighbor. On the contrary, the kingdom will rejoice if a new soul comes to know Christ in my house, messy or not. Mary had it right because she craved Jesus' teaching to the exclusion of all else. She wasn't being lazy or purposely ignoring her sister. She was sitting at the feet of the Lord Jesus Christ, soaking up his love and teaching.

1 Corinthians 12:4-11

There are different kinds of gifts, but the same Spirit. There are different kinds of service, but the same Lord. There are different kinds of working, but the same God works all of them in all men. Now to each one the manifestation of the Spirit is given for the common good. To one there is given through the Spirit the message of wisdom, to another the message of knowledge by means of the same Spirit, to another faith by the same Spirit, to another gifts of healing by that one Spirit, to another miraculous powers, to another prophecy, to another distinguishing between spirits, to another speaking in different kinds of tongues, and to still another the interpretation of tongues. All these are the work of one and the same Spirit, and he gives them to each one, just as he determines. (NIV)

Do we all have the same job as Christians? Why are they different?

How do we look at others with jobs and gifts that are different from ours?

This list of gifts can be a little stressful for us to read sometimes. What if our particular gift isn't on the list? Does that mean we're not gifted? No, it means that our gift isn't on this list. There are other places in the Bible that talk about spiritual gifts, but none of them are exhaustive. You won't find all the gifts God gives mentioned in a list. But if you open yourself to Him and His divine will, He can help you figure out your particular gifts and how you can use them for God's purposes.

We all have spiritual work, service, and gifts given to us by God that we are responsible for. He gives us these things individually which means that mine are going to be different from yours and yours are going to be different from your neighbor's, and so on. No matter the gift or work we have, we are to go about it in a Godly manner, always putting His needs first. Paul is telling us here to let God work through us. We are all going to serve and work differently, but it's all to the glory of his kingdom. You have specific gifts and jobs given to you by your Creator, and he holds you responsible for them.

What work has God given you to do? What gifts has he given you to accomplish this work?

What keeps you from doing your spiritual work, if anything?

Colossians 3:23-24

Whatever you do, work at it with all your heart, as working for the Lord, not for men, since you know that you will receive an inheritance from the Lord as a reward. It is the Lord Christ you are serving. (NIV)

What does this passage tell you about your work for the Lord?

Why is important to you?

How will your attitude at work (either a job or at home) change if you keep these verses in mind when you're working?

How can your life change if you make these verses your motto for working?

I think this is a good summary of why we should work hard at whatever we do. Do it for the Lord. Whatever it is – housework, a job, running a business – work at it with all your heart; do it for the Lord, and your reward will be great.

Think about how we can change the world simply by changing our attitudes. What kind of impact can you have on your boss or coworkers if you go to work every day to glorify God? What kind of impact can you have on your children if you wake up every day to glorify God as their mother? Whatever your work is, work at it with ALL your heart. Serve the Lord while you're doing it and your life will be different.

Think about the impact we can have on our families by living out this passage every day. Work for the Lord in everything you do – work, dishes, laundry, vacuuming, story time, bath time, etc. Your children and husband will notice, and you will exact change in your family. What a testament to God that will be!

Concluding Remarks

We all have work to do, and God is waiting for us to do it. Are you unsure what your work for the Lord is? Spend some time in prayer with God, and see what answer you get. You can be certain that he has a specific task for you, based on your talents and gifts, and he expects you to use it for His glory.

Don't let the challenges defeat you. Let them spur you on to greater things. Throw yourself into your work and see what spiritual benefits you will reap. God is ready and willing to help you with your tasks, whatever they may be. Let him in and watch your world change.

What are some things you are going to try to do differently to work for the Lord?

What do you think your biggest challenge will be?

Challenge

Read 1 Corinthians 12:4-11 and Romans 12:1-8. If you haven't determined your spiritual gifts yet, take some time to do so. Write them down and include some ideas on how you can use them to work for God. If you have trouble coming up with a list, ask a Christian sister to help. Sometimes others see our gifts more clearly than we ever will.

Chapter 6
An Energetic Woman

Objective: To learn what the Bible teaches about being energetic Christian women and why it's important. Compare and contrast God's viewpoints on energetic vs. lazy people. Learn how we can be more energetic, both physically and spiritually.

Energetic

How many of you automatically think of aerobics videos when you think about energetic women? Anyone who can bounce around for an hour with a smile screams energy, right? Children also come to mind when we think about energetic people. I don't know how many times I've felt like my children suck all the energy from me and channel it into themselves. As moms, energy is something we fondly remember possessing before we had children, and it's something we hope will come back as we get older.

What comes to mind when I say spiritual energy? Vortexes? Crystals? Earth mothers? We have grown up in a culture that takes spiritual energy to mean a mystical connection between the mind and the universe. I happen to believe in a different kind of spiritual energy – the energy you expend for the kingdom of God and for your own spiritual growth in Christ.

Let's continue to stretch our brains a little, and picture someone you consider lazy. This is a term we usually relate to solely on the physical level, even though it is often easier for people to be spiritually lazy than it is to be physically lazy. Many people will force themselves to get up and stay busy at their work but won't force themselves to get up and go to church, attend Bible study, or read their Bibles at home.

The Proverbs 31 Woman had no problems with energy. She was the epitome of an energetic woman, and she would have to be to maintain her crazy schedule! Between getting up early, conducting business, caring for her family and the poor, and whatever other day-to-day tasks popped up, she was running all day.

Does this sound familiar? Of course it does. We could easily insert ourselves into this picture. We all have different activities that fill our days, but I think we can relate to her schedule. As I've been saying, she was just a woman living her life, but living it for the Lord. We have access to the same energy she did – God – the wellspring of life itself. With his help, we can learn how to be more energetic for our families, our friends, and his kingdom.

Definitions

Energetic is defined as:

1)   : operating with or marked by vigor or effect

2)   : marked by <u>energy</u> : <u>strenuous</u> <an *energetic* walk>

3)   : of or relating to energy <*energetic* equation>

(<u>www.merriam-webster.com/dictionary/energetic</u>)

Lazy is defined as:

1)   *a* : disinclined to activity or exertion : not energetic or vigorous

b : encouraging inactivity or indolence <a *lazy* summer day>

2)   : moving slowly : <u>sluggish</u>

3)   : <u>droopy</u>, <u>lax</u> <a rabbit with *lazy* ears>

4)   : placed on its side <*lazy* E livestock brand>

5)   : not rigorous or strict <*lazy* scholarship>

(<u>www.merriam-webster.com/dictionary/lazy</u>)

Most of us know what it means to be energetic or to have the energy we need to complete a task. We also know what it means to be lazy. We will focus on applying the terms to our spiritual lives in this study. We rarely talk about being energetic or lazy Christians, but I think we can benefit from exploring the concept more. We're also going to talk about the effect that being physically energetic can have on your spiritual energy level, and vice versa. These two aspects of our lives are intrinsically connected and affect everything we do.

Proverbs 31:13-22; 27

She selects wool and flax and works with eager hands. She is like the merchant ships, bringing her food from afar. She gets up while it is still dark; she provides food for her family and portions for her servant girls. She considers a field and buys it; out of her earnings she plants a vineyard. She sets about her work vigorously; her arms are strong for her tasks. She sees that her trading is profitable, and her lamp does not go out at night. In her hand she holds the distaff and grasps the spindle with her fingers. She opens her arms to the poor and extends her hands to the needy. When it snows, she has no fear for her household; for all of them are clothed in scarlet. She makes coverings for her bed; she is clothed in fine linen and purple. (NIV)

She watches over the affairs of her household and does not eat the bread of idleness. (NIV)

What does the Proverbs 31 Woman do with her energy?

Do you think she struggled with finding the energy to complete her tasks? Why or why not?

Why should we avoid being idle?

I don't know about you, but reading through this list makes me kind of tired. It amazes me how much this woman managed to accomplish in a day. Sometimes I feel like I spend the day spinning my wheels between tasks and never get anything done. Do you ever feel that way?

I think that those days are going to happen, no matter who you are. We all have "off" days when nothing goes right and nothing gets done. We all get sick, or our kids get sick, or any number of other crazy things happen that zap our energy level. It's OK to have those days!

The Proverbs 31 Woman had those days, too, if she was a wife and mother (which she was.) But she didn't let those hiccups dictate her life. It's easy to let an illness or responsibility become an easy excuse for why we never get anything accomplished.

When those times come upon us, we have to remember to turn to the Lord and ask for help. We need to tap into the ultimate power source, and absorb the energy we need to be the best wives, moms, and women we can be.

What are some practical things you can do to make sure you have the energy you need to complete your tasks?

Proverbs 10:4; Proverbs 12:24

Lazy hands make a man poor, but diligent hands bring wealth. (NIV)

Diligent hands will rule, but laziness ends in slave labor. (NIV)

What warnings does the writer give here and why?

Why do you think the Proverbs writer addressed the issue?

Why does being lazy or diligent matter?

Passages like these appear throughout the book of Proverbs. It's almost like the writer wanted to make sure readers really got the concept down, so he tried to think of several ways to restate the same facts. If you can't grasp one idea, maybe another will make more sense to you. Both of these passages are clear: diligence (persistence or hard work) will be rewarded, and laziness will bring harm.

God wants us to be active workers in his kingdom. This is not a concept that has changed since the beginning of time. Adam was given work to do in the Garden of Eden, and we've all been given jobs of varying types ever since. As with so many things, being energetic is often a conscious choice we have to make in our lives.

We have to wake up every day and decide how active we're going to be – physically and spiritually. Are we going to exercise today? Are we going to write ourselves a "to-do" list and actually finish the things on it? Are we going to read the Bible or fellowship with other Christians? Are we going to talk to that neighbor who asked about church last week? These are all things we can control.

Maybe we can't exercise today due to an injury or ailment, but we plan for it tomorrow. We don't put it off indefinitely because that would have negative impacts on our physical health and energy.

It's the same with our spiritual activity level. We can't put off reading our Bible indefinitely if we want to maintain a healthy level of spiritual energy. We can't ignore other people in this world because we are too spiritually tired to help. God will give us the energy we need if we reach out and ask for it.

1 Corinthians 9:24-27

Do you not know that in a race all the runners run, but only one gets the prize? Run in such a way as to get the prize. Everyone who competes in the games goes into strict training. They do it to get a crown that will not last; but we do it to get a crown that will last forever. Therefore I do not run like a man running aimlessly; I do not fight like a man beating the air. No, I beat my body and make it my slave so that after I have preached to others, I myself will not be disqualified for the prize. (NIV)

Is this passage talking about physical activity, spiritual activity, or both? Why or why not?

What does this passage have to do with being energetic or lazy?

What does this passage mean for you personally?

This is a great passage for those of us who love to exercise. Those of us who do not would prefer to skip it, right? The truth of the matter is this passage is for both types of people. The passage is actually talking about our spiritual race using running as an analogy. Have you ever thought of your spiritual life as a race before? Do you think your attitude toward things might change if you approached your spiritual life like you do a 5K? We should be just as passionate about training our spiritual self as we are about training our physical self.

Well, what if we aren't passionate about training our bodies? We don't have to deal with that since it's not in the passage, right? Wrong!

We don't all love exercise, and that's OK. However, God expects us to care for the bodies he has given us (they are his temple, after all) and that means we need some sort of physical activity and healthy food. Refer back to the verses we read earlier in this lesson. God wants us to be diligent like the Proverbs 31 Woman was diligent. Did she have a gym membership or regular exercise routine? No, but she had a full life that kept her active and healthy. That's what he wants from us.

If our job doesn't give us the physical activity we need to stay healthy, then we need to find it elsewhere. Our physical energy level often relates to our physical health – we have less energy when we're unhealthy. We want to serve God to the best of our abilities which means we keep the physical vessel in good health as well as the spiritual.

I love the analogies Paul uses in these passages. Our spiritual walks should rival a race more than a leisurely stroll, shouldn't they? If you're preparing your heart every day so that it's ready to win your spiritual race, you'll put yourself in a good place to reach others for Christ. If you find yourself strolling along the spiritual boulevard wandering aimlessly, then maybe it's time to start training.

Matthew 14:12-14

John's disciples came and took his body and buried it. Then they went and told Jesus. When Jesus heard what had happened, he withdrew by boat privately to a solitary place. Hearing of this, the crowds followed him on foot from the towns. When Jesus landed and saw a large crowd, he had compassion on them and healed their sick. (NIV)

What do you think Jesus' energy level was at this point? Why?

How does he react when people still need him during a rough personal time?

How do you react to others' need for you during times of personal crisis?

You might be wondering why I included this passage in a study about being energetic. It doesn't seem to fit, does it? I admit, it's a little tricky, but it definitely fits in our study. Matthew 14:1-11 is the accounting of John the Baptist's death. We know from earlier in Matthew that Jesus and John the Baptist were related, and Jesus had just learned of John's horrible death at the hands of Herod. He was grieving and emotionally spent. He just wanted to get away to a quiet place where he could restore his spirit, but people followed.

Stop for a second and put yourself in his place. Have you lost a loved one? Most of us have lost someone close to us, either friend or family. You know how it rips you apart inside. Now, imagine having people surrounding you who need something from you. They're offering no comfort to you; no respite from the pain – just raw, human need. How do you react?

Jesus reacted with compassion and love. He put his need secondary to theirs and stood ready to serve. Even in his low times, Jesus found the energy to minister to those who needed him.

That's what I want us to take away from this passage. Even during our low points, Jesus can provide the energy we need to complete our tasks, both physical and spiritual. It's not easy, and it wasn't easy on Jesus, but he did it anyway. Sometimes we just have to do it anyway. Even when we're hurting and down, people are going to need us and we need to be ready to serve them.

Just like Christ, we have a Heavenly Father who stands ready and willing to provide us the energy we need to serve others, especially when we feel it flagging within ourselves. I think we'll be pleasantly surprised if we test Him in this. He will grant the energy we need - we just have to ask.

Hebrews 6:10-12

God is not unjust; he will not forget your work and the love you have shown him as you have helped his people and continue to help them. We want each of you to show this same diligence to the very end, in order to make your hope sure. We do not want you to become lazy, but to imitate those who through faith and patience inherit what has been promised. (NIV)

What does this passage teach you about spiritual energy?

Why do you think the Hebrew author is cautioning Christians about being lazy?

What are some of the problems we see in churches today due to Christians' laziness?

I find it interesting that the Hebrew writer is reminding his audience that God is just and will reward them for the work they're doing. Isn't that still true today? We want to work hard and receive our reward for that hard work. I find that I have more energy for a job when I reap some kind of reward for it, be that physical or spiritual. I think the writer is saying that if we continue to devote our energies to the building of the kingdom, our reward waits for us in heaven.

I think he cautioned against spiritual laziness because of the results it produces. What impact on the world will spiritually lazy Christians have? Nothing positive; it's hard to positively impact anyone when you're not willing to expend energy for them.

Isn't it interesting that he combines thoughts of laziness with faith and hope? They don't seem to go together, but Paul clearly stitches them together. What he's saying is don't quit working just because it gets hard – hold on to the faith and hope of Jesus Christ, and you will reap your reward in heaven. Isn't that a great encouragement for us?

Is there anything in particular that is keeping you from expending spiritual energy? What can you do about it?

2 Thessalonians 3:11-13

We hear that some among you are idle. They are not busy; they are busybodies. Such people we command and urge in the Lord Jesus Christ to settle down and earn the bread they eat. And as for you, brothers, never tire of doing what is right.
(NIV)

What problems can busybodies cause in the church?

Why do you think Paul is warning against idleness and busybodies?

How do you contribute to busybody troubles in your church?

We've all known them – the eternal busybodies of the church who have their noses in everyone's business and are happy to share that information with everyone around them. Imagine for a moment if these people chose to expend that energy in a positive manner to build up those around them. What would the impact be? Our churches would be so much stronger if we worked together at building the body and quit focusing so much on tearing it down.

I included this passage for a few reasons: first, it's important to note that the early church struggled with lazy Christians, just like we do today; second, we should note that idleness in our spiritual lives is not acceptable and leads to bad behavior; third, we should never tire of doing what is right. No matter what other people are doing or not doing, we should never tire of doing what's right. If our hearts are focused on God, and we're drawing our energy from him, who can stop us?

It's a simple few verses, but it contains some sobering teaching for each one of us. What if we're the busybody in our church? How do we fix it? Paul answers that question for us. Settle down, work hard, and strive to do what is right. It's not complicated if we let these verses serve as our template.

What if we're dealing with a busybody? Do what is right tirelessly - in other words, don't stoop to their level and wade into the muck. Do what God wants you to do and provide a good example for others around you.

Galatians 2:20

I have been crucified with Christ and I no longer live, but Christ lives in me. The life I live in the body, I live by faith in the Son of God, who loved me and gave himself for me. (NIV)

What does this passage have to do with energy?

Can this passage help you be more energetic, either spiritually or physically? Why or why not?

What do you think your biggest challenge will be?

The message in this passage is beautiful to me. Our lives changed when Jesus took up residence. We now live for him, and he lives in us. It puts a different perspective on our energy problem, doesn't it? If Christ is living in us, we have limitless energy to draw from to keep us strong and energetic in our Christian walk.

Even on our bad days, physically and spiritually, Jesus provides for us. When he lives in us, we have access to him each and every day. This passage means a lot to me when I'm having a bad day with my back because I know that even though I hurt physically, Jesus is with me at all times. I may be unable to get out and exercise on those days, but I can spend extra time in my devotions with him which isn't a bad trade off.

Concluding Remarks

We all have such power and energy at our fingertips, ready and waiting for us if we will just ask for it. We know that we have work to do, and now we know the kind of energy he has given us to do it. What's stopping us now?

I hope you can see how important the bond between physical and spiritual energy is in your life. Do you notice that you feel more positive after exercise? I certainly do, and it often helps me clear my head when I need to sit and write or edit for several hours.

Conversely, when my spirit exercises regularly, physical things flow smoothly. For instance, when I focus on my relationship with Christ, my physical stresses like pain, budgetary issues, and personal relationships are easier to deal with. It's not an accident that things work this way. God knows what he's doing – he knows what we need to stay both physically and spiritually energetic, and he provides everything we need to make it happen. We just have to be energetic.

Challenge

Read 1 Corinthians 9:24 - 27 again. Think about how this passage can apply to you and your spiritual energy. **Brainstorm your ideas here. Pick one idea and work on making it a reality in your life. Feel free to journal your successes and failures below.**

Chapter 7
A Wise Woman

Objective: To learn why we should seek wisdom in our lives. Learn the benefits of wisdom as wives, mothers, and friends. Learn why God wants us to be wise and how we accomplish it.

Wisdom

Does anything in particular jump into your head when you hear the term wisdom? Who do you think of? Now visualize a wise woman. What do you see? An old crone, white witch, or village healer? We don't often refer to women in our culture today as wise, but rather discerning or perceptive; someone with understanding and good judgment. Does this change your mental picture? We often think wisdom belongs to the old or the super-intelligent, not something available to us normal folks, but that's not the case.

We all know smart people, but what is it that makes someone wise? A wise person has something extra – that little bit of extra spark that makes their intelligence real and vibrant. The wise person is who we want to ask and take advice from. Wisdom doesn't require a high IQ or several college degrees. Any one of us can become wise if we want to expend the effort into becoming so.

The Proverbs 31 Woman was a wise woman. She was that person people could come to for advice and receive a straight answer. I like to think that she was an approachable woman who didn't intimidate people with her knowledge but offered her help freely to whoever needed it.

We have already studied many of this woman's characteristics, and her wisdom shines through every aspect of her life. Because she possessed Godly wisdom, she was able to maintain self-control, virtue, kindness, compassion, and energy as she went about her day-to-day life. Is this something you would like to see in your life? Wouldn't it be nice to possess a Godly wisdom that would help you make good decisions for your family?

Definitions

The definition of **wise** is:

1) *a* : characterized by wisdom : marked by deep understanding, keen discernment, and a capacity for sound judgment
   b : exercising or showing sound judgment : <u>prudent</u> <a *wise* investor>
2) *a* : evidencing or hinting at the possession of inside information : <u>knowing</u>
   b : possessing inside information <the police got *wise* to his whereabouts>
   c : <u>crafty</u>, <u>shrewd</u>
   d : aware of or informed about a particular matter —usually used in the comparative in negative constructions with *the* <was none the *wiser* about their plans>
3) *archaic* : skilled in magic or divination
4) : <u>insolent</u>, <u>smart-alecky</u>, <u>fresh</u> <a tough kid with a *wise* mouth>
(<u>www.merriam-webster.com/dictionary/wise</u>)

Wisdom is defined as:

1) *a* : accumulated philosophic or scientific learning : <u>knowledge</u>
   b : ability to discern inner qualities and relationships : <u>insight</u>
   c : good sense : <u>judgment</u>
   d : generally accepted belief <challenges what has become accepted *wisdom* among many historians — Robert Darnton>
2) : a wise attitude, belief, or course of action
3) : the teachings of the ancient wise men
(<u>www.merriam-webster.com/dictionary/wisdom</u>)

There's a lot of useful material in these definitions. Read through them again and pay special attention to the traits used in the definitions: understanding, discernment, judgment, prudent, knowing, crafty, shrewd, insight. These are things we understand more in our world today. We can identify more with these terms and use them to fully understand what the Bible is teaching us about wisdom.

Proverbs 31:25-31; 10-12

She is clothed with strength and dignity; she can laugh at the days to come. She speaks with wisdom, and faithful instruction is on her tongue. She watches over the affairs of her household and does not eat the bread of idleness. Her children arise and call her blessed; her husband also, and he praises her: "Many women do noble things, but you surpass them all." Charm is deceptive, and beauty is fleeting; but a woman who fears the LORD is to be praised. Give her the reward she has earned, and let her works bring her praise at the city gate. (NIV)

A wife of noble character who can find? She is worth far more than rubies. Her husband has full confidence in her and lacks nothing of value. She brings him good, not harm, all the days of her life. (NIV)

Why is wisdom an important characteristic for the Proverbs 31 Woman to possess?

What are some ways you can think of that wisdom would benefit her in her life?

What areas of her life were affected by her wisdom?

What areas of your life do you need wisdom in right now?

This can be an overwhelming passage for us. Not only does the Proverbs 31 Woman get everything under the sun accomplished in her life, she also does it with wisdom, grace, and panache. We might as well throw in the towel now, right? Wrong! We have access to the same well she did – God – and he has provided access to wisdom for us all, if we're willing to take hold of it.

If you read the passage carefully, you can see where her wisdom comes from – fear of the Lord. As we learned in our first lesson, fearing God is the foundation of all our Christian attributes. Without a healthy, reverent awe for the Creator, you can't grow in your faith and become wise in his ways. The Proverbs 31 Woman wasn't relying on her own wisdom and all-around awesomeness to accomplish all that she did. She relied on God and let him help her through her days.

Do you think you can let God help you become wise? It's not easy to set yourself aside and allow him to work through you. But the results are worth it. I can just imagine a world filled with wise women of God. Wouldn't it be beautiful?

Proverbs 9

Invitations of Wisdom and of Folly

Wisdom has built her house; she has hewn out its seven pillars. She has prepared her meat and mixed her wine; she has also set her table. She has sent out her maids, and she calls from the highest point of the city. "Let all who are simple come in here!" she says to those who lack judgment. "Come, eat my food and drink the wine I have mixed. Leave your simple ways and you will live; walk in the way of understanding." Whoever corrects a mocker invites insult; whoever rebukes a wicked man incurs abuse. Do not rebuke a mocker or he will hate you; rebuke a wise man and he will love you. Instruct a wise man and he will be wiser still; teach a righteous man and he will add to his learning. "The fear of the LORD is the beginning of wisdom, and knowledge of the Holy One is understanding. For through me your days will be many, and years will be added to your life. If you are wise, your wisdom will reward you; if you are a mocker, you alone will suffer." The woman Folly is loud; she is undisciplined and without knowledge. She sits at the door of her house, on a seat at the highest point of the city, calling out to those who pass by, who go straight on their way. "Let all who are simple come in here!" she says to those who lack judgment. "Stolen water is sweet; food eaten in secret is delicious!" But little do they know that the dead are there, that her guests are in the depths of the grave. (NIV)

What do you think of this passage?

What does Wisdom offer us? What does Folly offer?

Do you ever feel the tug of war between these two virtues in your life? Which one usually wins?

Why do we choose the way of Folly? What about it makes it look tempting?

I love this passage! The pictures of Wisdom and Folly are so clear and sobering. Wisdom has planned ahead, prepared her feast, and sent servants out to find guests. She herself is calling to those who need her most. She's not frantic about anything because she prepared for contingencies ahead of time. She's not shy about what she's offering, but she's not going to force it on anyone either. She's offering a better life, but it's one that requires thinking, planning, and good judgment. Yes, it's fulfilling and full of eternal reward, but it's hard work.

Have you ever stopped to think about what it means to: *"walk in the way of understanding?"* It's a simple phrase that means a lot to Christians who want to be wise. The passage goes on to say: *"The fear of the LORD is the beginning of wisdom, and knowledge of the Holy One is understanding."* Knowledge of God and his ways brings us to understanding, and fearing him brings wisdom.

Folly, on the other hand, didn't bother to plan for anything. She's loud, ignorant, undisciplined, and too lazy to leave her comfortable seat. She just yells out from her chair and waits for the naïve, lazy, and stupid to head her way. Sadly, she will probably have better attendance at her feast because she doesn't require anything – come satisfy your baser urges, and forget all about any kind of responsibility or hard work. Isn't that tempting sometimes? Don't you want to leave your responsibilities behind and just forget them all, especially when times are tough? Unfortunately, those who join in her feast don't realize that they're doing so at their own peril.

This is a good picture of Christianity compared to the world. Christ offers us wisdom, but we have to reach for it and take it from him. Satan offers us anything our hearts desire for the short term – but the payment is our soul. As Christians, we sometimes lament that we don't get to have any "fun," even though that fun lasts a short time and puts our souls at risk. Why is it that we don't look at those people engaging in such dangerous behavior with sadness and pity? Because at heart, we still want to play both sides – wisdom and folly. We want wisdom on Sundays when we go to church, but we want folly on Friday night when we go out partying.

God doesn't work this way. When we choose him he expects to see a change, and so do those around us. Non-Christians often watch us to see if we act differently from other people they know. When we choose wisdom instead of folly we have a real chance to make a difference to those around us who are watching.

Proverbs 2:1-15

My son, if you accept my words and store up my commands within you, turning your ear to wisdom and applying your heart to understanding, and if you call out for insight and cry aloud for understanding, and if you look for it as for silver and search for it as for hidden treasure, then you will understand the fear of the LORD and find the knowledge of God. For the LORD gives wisdom, and from his mouth come knowledge and understanding. He holds victory in store for the upright, he is a shield to those whose walk is blameless, for he guards the course of the just and protects the way of his faithful ones. Then you will understand what is right and just and fair--every good path. For wisdom will enter your heart, and knowledge will be pleasant to your soul. Discretion will protect you, and understanding will guard you. Wisdom will save you from the ways of wicked men, from men whose words are perverse, who leave the straight paths to walk in dark ways, who delight in doing wrong and rejoice in the perverseness of evil, whose paths are crooked and who are devious in their ways. (NIV)

What is the relationship between wisdom and fearing the Lord?

How can wisdom benefit you in your life today?

This passage gives us some insights on wisdom and how much we should want to have it. Imagine searching for wisdom like hidden treasure – the excitement, the joy, the fun! This is the attitude we should have about attaining wisdom. It should be the "X" on our treasure map, the chest of jewels that we can't wait to break open. Do we ever look at wisdom this way? Have you ever applied yourself to gaining wisdom in the same way you apply yourself to looking for a new home or finding a lost piece of jewelry? Imagine the benefits for your life if you decided today to seek wisdom out like the Proverbs writer says here. What a beautiful gift it would be!

Look at the other rich blessings offered by choosing wisdom: knowledge, understanding, and discernment. I think we forget that wisdom is an important part of being a mature Christian. The kingdom of God doesn't exist because of the hard work and sacrifice of fools, but on the hard work, sacrifice, and dedication of men and women who chose God's wisdom over that of the world. Don't you want to be a Christian who chooses wisdom and gains understanding and discernment? I know I do.

I keep going back to two particular sentences in this passage: *"For wisdom will enter your heart, and knowledge will be pleasant to your soul. Discretion will protect you, and understanding will guard you."* Have you ever considered that wisdom can protect you? These are the words we need to write on our hearts every day, especially when we falter in our walk. All of these things provide protection to our hearts as we interact in the world, and they will help us show God to those around us.

Wisdom and knowledge are available to us; they will live inside us, in fact, if we choose to let them in. How? By opening your heart to God and accepting his teaching and commands. Let him share his understanding with you, and his wisdom will dwell in your heart and protect your soul.

Matthew 7:24-27

The Wise and Foolish Builders

"Therefore everyone who hears these words of mine and puts them into practice is like a wise man who built his house on the rock. The rain came down, the streams rose, and the winds blew and beat against that house; yet it did not fall, because it had its foundation on the rock. But everyone who hears these words of mine and does not put them into practice is like a foolish man who built his house on sand. The rain came down, the streams rose, and the winds blew and beat against that house, and it fell with a great crash." (NIV)

What is the meaning of this parable?

What foundation should we build on?

What does this passage mean for you personally?

Every time I read this passage, I think of the children's song, "The Wise Man Built His House." My girls all loved to sing it when they were little, especially the part where the foolish man's house goes "SPLAT!" It's cute and funny when we sing it in a little song, but think about what this parable is talking about. Those of us who build on a foundation of Jesus Christ won't fall in the storms of life because our foundation is solid. But those who build on a faulty foundation (atheism, evolution, etc.) won't survive the storms of life. Pretty sobering, isn't it?

I think it's also important to point out the fact that having a solid foundation does not protect you from getting through the storm. God doesn't promise us smooth sailing or perfect lives – he, in fact, promises the opposite. But we are promised a firm foundation to stand on when those hurricanes of trial come knocking. I don't know about you, but I gain a lot of comfort from that. I know I can't stand by myself against trials, but knowing Christ is with me through everything I go through gives me confidence and strength.

So, what does this passage teach us about being wise? It's simple: if we choose God's wisdom and his firm foundation, we'll weather the storms of life in one piece; if we choose the world's wisdom and faulty foundation, we'll fall apart in the storms we encounter. As we read in Proverbs, Godly wisdom will protect our souls from the dangers all around us. This is especially important when the storm is raging all around us, and we're faltering. We can always reach out for our Savior in the storm, and he will reach down and help us through it.

James 3:13-18

Who is wise and understanding among you? Let him show it by his good life, by deeds done in the humility that comes from wisdom. But if you harbor bitter envy and selfish ambition in your hearts, do not boast about it or deny the truth. Such "wisdom" does not come down from heaven but is earthly, unspiritual, of the devil. For where you have envy and selfish ambition, there you find disorder and every evil practice. But the wisdom that comes from heaven is first of all pure; then peace-loving, considerate, submissive, full of mercy and good fruit, impartial and sincere. Peacemakers who sow in peace raise a harvest of righteousness. (NIV)

What does wisdom from heaven look like?

What does man's wisdom look like?

What happens in our lives when we choose man's wisdom over God's? What happens when we choose God's wisdom instead of man's?

How would our churches change if more people chose heavenly wisdom over man's wisdom?

James had such a way with words, didn't he? He was a straightforward writer, and he certainly didn't shy away from tough topics. I appreciate the pictures of Godly wisdom versus man's wisdom in this passage. It gives us a clear picture of what we should be striving toward and what we need to avoid at all costs in our spiritual walks.

We learn a lot about why God wants us to be wise in this passage. First, we see what earthly wisdom gets us – a whole lot of trouble and alliance with Satan – you can't continue in your evil ways if you're full of God and his Spirit. God wants us to choose his wisdom because it's transforming. Instead of selfish ambition, envy, and evil, we exhibit peace, purity, submission, consideration, and mercy which lead us to righteousness. Godly wisdom helps us become right with God. If you're relying on God to show you what matters, your life is going to be pointing more in his direction.

It's still up to you to choose your direction, though. You have to be the one to reach out and choose to follow him, taking up your cross every day, and living your life in a way that his light shines through.

Imagine what our churches could accomplish if all Christians suddenly decided to adopt this passage as a way of life. We would be such a force for Christ, working together for the good of his kingdom instead of getting mired in petty arguments and ego contests. We would be unstoppable.

2 Timothy 3:10-17

You, however, know all about my teaching, my way of life, my purpose, faith, patience, love, endurance, persecutions, sufferings--what kinds of things happened to me in Antioch, Iconium and Lystra, the persecutions I endured. Yet the Lord rescued me from all of them. In fact, everyone who wants to live a godly life in Christ Jesus will be persecuted, while evil men and impostors will go from bad to worse, deceiving and being deceived. But as for you, continue in what you have learned and have become convinced of, because you know those from whom you learned it, and how from infancy you have known the holy Scriptures, which are able to make you wise for salvation through faith in Christ Jesus. All Scripture is God-breathed and is useful for teaching, rebuking, correcting and training in righteousness, so that the man of God may be thoroughly equipped for every good work. (NIV)

What does this passage teach you about wisdom and where we find it?

What things are we promised in this passage? Are they all good things?

What simple thing can you do to gain Godly wisdom?

Who knew that obtaining wisdom could be as simple as cracking open the Bible and delving into Scripture? I think we often forget that God has left us everything we need to know him and develop our relationship with him in the Bible. It's THE ULTIMATE self-help book.

It's also important to realize that wisdom and faithfulness do not make us immune to troubles. They do, in fact, open us up to more persecution from Satan. The more Christians there are reading their Bibles and gaining Godly wisdom, the less power Satan has over us, and the more he is going to increase his attacks against us. Do you think we can learn to rejoice over the increased attacks? Maybe we should consider it a blessing.

I love the picture Paul creates here of Scripture. God breathed it - his very essence inhabits the pages of our Bibles, and he's provided us a way to come closer to him through those pages. Look at what Scripture is good for: teaching, rebuking, correcting, and training in righteousness. That pretty much covers the whole spectrum, doesn't it?

God's word will help us in every part of our lives - it will teach us, it will how us when we're wrong and convict our hearts, and it will train us in righteousness. What more do we need?

It's so important to read the Bible and learn more about God and his plan. He has revealed himself to us in so many ways throughout both the Old and New Testaments, and it's exciting to delve into it and get to know him better. If you find yourself confused or troubled, I encourage you to ask questions of a trusted spiritual advisor: your minister, husband, parents, or best friend. Don't quit! He has so much to teach you.

James 1:2-5

Consider it pure joy, my brothers, whenever you face trials of many kinds, because you know that the testing of your faith develops perseverance. Perseverance must finish its work so that you may be mature and complete, not lacking anything. If any of you lacks wisdom, he should ask God, who gives generously to all without finding fault, and it will be given to him. (NIV)

How should we feel when we face trials?

What benefits can we reap by changing our outlook on trials and persecution?

How might your life change if you embrace this passage and live it every day?

This passage is so important for us to understand. It's one of the more difficult passages for us to digest because it's challenging. We have such a hard time finding joy in our trials, don't we? But look what we miss out on – perseverance, maturity, and completeness – if we don't endure trial. I don't know about you, but I want to be a complete Christian, and to be a complete Christian we have to learn to persevere. You can only learn to persevere if you have trials, so I guess we have to learn to deal with these trials that come to us.

What does wisdom have to do with all of this? It looks to me like wisdom ties in with perseverance and maturity, which makes sense. You can't be immature and wise together, can you? In order to be wise, you must be mature.

It makes me think of growing up. As teenagers, we want desperately to be mature and complete, but we're not; we can't be because we haven't been through the tough things in life that build character and maturity. It's a bit of a vicious circle, isn't it? If you want to be a mature, wise, complete Christian, you have to learn to accept your difficulties with a joyful spirit – look at them as an opportunity for growth instead of a punishment. Do you think this is something you can do?

I'm working on this in my own life. One thing I've learned in my journey is that God's plan for me and my life looks a lot different from the plan I laid out for myself, and I wouldn't have found my purpose without the trials I've had to go through. If I hadn't dealt with two back surgeries that laid me flat for months, I wouldn't have picked up my writing again, and I'd still be wandering around trying to figure out what to do with myself. But, because in the midst of that trial, I finally gave in and let him take over, he's been able to make my new path clear. He's blessed me over and over again with opportunities and inspiration, and I can now look back on those times and be joyful that I went through them.

Colossians 4:5-6

Be wise in the way you act toward outsiders; make the most of every opportunity. Let your conversation be always full of grace, seasoned with salt, so that you may know how to answer everyone. (NIV)

Why is it important to show wisdom when dealing with those outside the church?

What changes can we make in our lives if we learn to interact with others gracefully?

I think this is an interesting passage for us to wrap up our lesson with because it's deceptively short and simple. We read it and say to ourselves, "OK, that's easy. I can be nice to outsiders," and go about our business. Look again at what Paul says: we are to be wise in the way we interact with outsiders, and be ready for EVERY opportunity that arises. That means we need to make sure we prepare not only with the truth of God but also with a kind and compassionate manner toward those we're trying to reach. We need to tap into Godly wisdom and let it guide us in how we interact with others.

Concluding Remarks

As with so many things we have studied so far, we underestimate God's power and our abilities to tap into it. We read about people in the Bible without ever comparing our stories. I think it's important to remember that we are studying about real people who lived in a real world – surprisingly more similar to ours than you might think.

They needed Godly wisdom to interact with the world of their time just as badly as we need it to live in our world today. God's wisdom is waiting for you to reach out and take it. Remember Wisdom from the Proverb? You're going to have to take the steps toward God and his wisdom. He's generously offered it to you, but you are required to accept it. Are you willing to make the effort? A whole new world awaits you if you do.

Would you like to be wise as the Proverbs 31 Woman was wise? Why or why not?

How would your life change if you embraced the Godly wisdom offered in the Bible?

Challenge

Meditate on Godly wisdom for a moment. **How has God provided his wisdom to you? Have trials in your life brought you closer to spiritual maturity, or have they pulled you away from God? Read James 1:2-5 and 3:13-18 again. If your life is pulling you away from God, spend some time in prayer and reflection over it. I encourage you to reach out to God and let him work on healing your heart. If your life is pulling you toward God, spend some time thanking him for the opportunities he's provided. Re-dedicate yourself to the work he's given you to do.**

Chapter 8
A Loved Woman

Objective: To learn that we can all be loved women and why we want to be loved women. Learn that love is a gift we have been offered, and learn how we can fully take advantage of this gift. Learn what God wants us to do with this gift and how we can show his love to others.

Loved

You are loved. Did you know that? Even if you are still single, waiting for Prince Charming to come riding in on his steed, or if your Prince Charming rode away into the sunset, you are loved. You may be happily married with children and a minivan, but someone else loves you, too. Unconditionally and Completely.

"How?" you might ask. The Savior and Master of the Universe loves you. That's right – the most powerful, awesome, perfect God thinks you are worthy of his love. Wow! Isn't that amazing?

You might think I'm a little crazy for being so basic with this topic. But I think that we don't tap into God's love like we should, and I think we pay some serious consequences for that. Intellectually we know that God loves us – we sing songs about it all the time at church, right? But do you ever feel his arms close around you in comfort when things are going wrong? Is he the first one you go to with good news? Does he even make your list?

Americans as a whole are good at putting God up on a shelf and bringing him down a couple times a week (or year) before church. We miss out on so much love that he has for us because we don't even think to reach out and accept it from him. We don't crack open our Bibles to read the loving words he has for us because it's too hard or boring or was written for people thousands of years ago and is no longer relevant.

We're going to delve into the concept of love in this lesson in a way that you might not have explored before. I'm going to show you the love that's available and waiting for you, and we'll see how it can apply to your life.

I don't think anyone can say that the Proverbs 31 Woman was unloved. I think we would say just the opposite – this was a woman cherished not only by her husband and children, but also by her servants and the people in her community. Because of choices she made in her life: fearing the Lord, being kind and compassionate, responsible, energetic, wise, and self-controlled, she inspired love in those around her. We, too, can aspire to this. We can be women who inspire love everywhere we go. Wouldn't that be a nice reputation to have? I would love to be that woman.

Definitions

Love:

1) *a (1)* : strong affection for another arising out of kinship or personal ties <maternal *love* for a child>

    (2) : attraction based on sexual desire : affection and tenderness felt by <u>lovers</u>

    (3) : affection based on admiration, <u>benevolence</u>, or common interests <*love* for his old schoolmates>

    b : an assurance of affection <give her my *love*>

2) : warm <u>attachment</u>, enthusiasm, or devotion <*love* of the sea>

3) *a* : the object of attachment, devotion, or admiration <baseball was his first *love*>

    b (1) : a beloved person : <u>darling</u> —often used as a term of endearment

    (2) British —used as an informal term of address

4) a : unselfish loyal and benevolent concern for the good of another: as

    (1) : the fatherly concern of God for humankind

    (2) : brotherly concern for others

    b : a person's adoration of God

5) : a god or <u>personification</u> of love

6) : an <u>amorous</u> episode : <u>love affair</u>

7) : the sexual embrace : <u>copulation</u>

8) : a score of zero (as in tennis)

9) *capitalized Christian Science* : <u>god</u>

(<u>www.merriam-webster.com/dictionary/love</u>)

We tend to be comfortable with the idea of love in our society today. What I want you to take note of here are the different types of love you can exhibit. Isn't it amazing that God built us so that we can love those around us in so many ways?

Proverbs 31:28-31

Her children arise and call her blessed; her husband also, and he praises her: "Many women do noble things, but you surpass them all." Charm is deceptive, and beauty is fleeting; but a woman who fears the LORD is to be praised. Give her the reward she has earned, and let her works bring her praise at the city gate. (NIV)

How does this passage illustrate the Proverbs 31 Woman as loved?

How does this passage differ from our vision of a loved woman?

How would you feel if your husband and children referred to you this way?

Knowing what you do about the Proverbs 31 Woman, how do you think this would make her feel?

Our Proverbs 31 gal was indeed a loved woman, and this passage proves it. How many of you have husbands who praise you above all other women or children who call you blessed? I love the fact that Proverbs 31 ends with this passage. Wouldn't this be a great summation of a life lived for God and family? I would love to have my family feel this way at the end of the day.

Sometimes I think we get so caught up in hearing the words, "I love you," that we miss out on all the ways love can be expressed. Proverbs 31 does not refer to love by name, and yet it's everywhere in the passage: from the way our gal interacts with family, friends, her household, and the public, to the way her husband and children interact with her. It pervades this passage in a very real way that shows us her world was full of love.

Do you feel loved by your family or those close around you? Do you have someone in your life who values you above great treasures? If not, remember that God feels these things for you. He values you above all treasures - he gave his Son for you, after all!

At the end of the day, what matters is how we live our lives for God – not for other people or for accolades – so we should focus on making him the center of our lives.

Remember, the Proverbs 31 Woman lived her life with God at the center. Look again at our passage: *"...but a woman who fears the Lord is to be praised."* No matter what your personal situation is, God should be your center. Build your life on the fear of the Lord and see how he pours his love over you every day.

Psalm 103

Of David.

Praise the LORD, O my soul; all my inmost being, praise his holy name. Praise the LORD, O my soul, and forget not all his benefits-- who forgives all your sins and heals all your diseases, who redeems your life from the pit and crowns you with love and compassion, who satisfies your desires with good things so that your youth is renewed like the eagle's. The LORD works righteousness and justice for all the oppressed. He made known his ways to Moses, his deeds to the people of Israel: The LORD is compassionate and gracious, slow to anger, abounding in love. He will not always accuse, nor will he harbor his anger forever; he does not treat us as our sins deserve or repay us according to our iniquities. For as high as the heavens are above the earth, so great is his love for those who fear him; as far as the east is from the west, so far has he removed our transgressions from us. As a father has compassion on his children, so the LORD has compassion on those who fear him; for he knows how we are formed, he remembers that we are dust. As for man, his days are like grass, he flourishes like a flower of the field; the wind blows over it and it is gone, and its place remembers it no more. But from everlasting to everlasting the LORD's love is with those who fear him, and his righteousness with their children's children-- with those who keep his covenant and remember to obey his precepts. The LORD has established his throne in heaven, and his kingdom rules over all. Praise the LORD, you his angels, you mighty ones who do his bidding, who obey his word. Praise the LORD, all his heavenly hosts, you his servants who do his will. Praise the LORD, all his works everywhere in his dominion. Praise the LORD, O my soul. (NIV)

Describe God's love for us. Do you feel this in your life? Why or why not?

What does God do for those who love him?

How might your life change if you carry this knowledge in your heart every day?

What message can you take away from this psalm?

David really had a way with words, didn't he? You can feel his passion for God in each word of the psalms he wrote. This psalm is such a beautiful illustration of God's love for us: merciful, gracious, all-encompassing. There is nothing like God's love anywhere on this earth. Imagine for one moment the greatest love of your life. Do you realize that this love, no matter how perfect and wonderful, is nothing compared to the love God has for you?

David also reminds us in this psalm that God loves us as a father loves his children. For those of us who have loving fathers, this makes a lot of sense. I know how much my Dad loves me, and I know I'm important to him. It's fairly easy for me to think of God as my father because I have a good earthly example to look to.

But what do you do if your earthly father is cruel, violent, or evil? How do you equate God's love with what you've experienced from your father? In that situation, I would say that you need to think of God as everything your earthly father isn't. Your earthly father isn't kind – God is. Your earthly father doesn't care about your well-being – God cares about every hair on your head. God is everything you've ever dreamed a father would be, and he desperately wants to share his love with you. Where your earthly father has failed, God will prevail. As his daughter you'll never be disappointed.

Wrapped up in the all-encompassing love God has for us is his patience with our humanness. Even though we're like grass – here one day and gone the next – he values us and loves us from everlasting to everlasting. That's a lot of love! I don't know about you, but thinking about God's love and patience makes me want to work harder to please him. If he can love me knowing all the bad things I've done, I can work every day to make choices that glorify his name and build his kingdom.

John 3:16-21

"For God so loved the world that he gave his one and only Son, that whoever believes in him shall not perish but have eternal life. For God did not send his Son into the world to condemn the world, but to save the world through him. Whoever believes in him is not condemned, but whoever does not believe stands condemned already because he has not believed in the name of God's one and only Son. This is the verdict: Light has come into the world, but men loved darkness instead of light because their deeds were evil. Everyone who does evil hates the light, and will not come into the light for fear that his deeds will be exposed. But whoever lives by the truth comes into the light, so that it may be seen plainly that what he has done has been
done through God." (NIV)

What does this passage teach us about love?

What was God willing to sacrifice because of his love for us?

What, if anything, are you willing to sacrifice because of your love for God?

My girls have all memorized John 3:16 years ago for Bible classes. I love hearing them recite this verse, and I hope that it sinks in for them. It makes me wonder, though, does it sink in for me? How often do I sit back and reflect on God's love for me? Would I be willing to sacrifice one of my children to save someone else? I don't know if I can answer that question.

Now, granted, sacrificing one of my children is not going to bring about the salvation of the world, but put yourself in God's place for one minute. The only way he could redeem a fallen creation was to send Jesus, his Son, a part of him, to a world that was going to use and abuse him – and kill him. But we don't see him hemming and hawing and being indecisive. He sent his perfect Son here to live life as a perfect man and then die a horrible, painful death as a criminal on a cross so that we can have the option to choose him.

It sure puts things in perspective, doesn't it? We're so cavalier with our relationship with God. We read the Bible when it suits us, or leave it on the shelf when it doesn't. We may talk about church with someone, if it's convenient or comfortable, but not if it makes us nervous. What would we ever do if God decided to approach our relationship this way? Aren't you thankful that God doesn't love you with the standards of this world?

I'm afraid to think of what that would look like in my life. I've taken God for granted or pulled him out when it's convenient so many times. Thank the Lord that he doesn't love like we do! If it was up to us to provide a sacrifice for the world, the world would stand condemned. I think it's time for us to get real about God's love – God's love for us is active, living, and unending. Shouldn't you reciprocate?

John 15:12-17

My command is this: Love each other as I have loved you. Greater love has no one than this, that he lay down his life for his friends. You are my friends if you do what I command. I no longer call you servants, because a servant does not know his master's business. Instead, I have called you friends, for everything that I learned from my Father I have made known to you. You did not choose me, but I chose you and appointed you to go and bear fruit--fruit that will last. Then the Father will give you whatever you ask in my name. This is my command: Love each other. (NIV)

What does this passage mean to you?

How does Jesus expect us to love each other?

How does Jesus' command differ from the worlds'?

What does friendship with Christians look like when we follow Jesus' commands in this passage?

The book of John is full of such useful Christian wisdom. We've already read about God's love for us in the beginning of this study, now we get a chance to learn how God would have us love others. He gives us a wonderful opportunity. Not only has he made his love for us so visible through scripture, he's also given us clear directions on how we can in turn show that love to each other.

Christian love isn't about soft feelings and shallow relationships. It involves self-sacrifice, compassion, and obedience to God's plan. We don't get up every day and wonder what our friends will do for us; we get up every day ready to serve those around us and do whatever it takes to help them find Christ for themselves.

How often do you think about giving up your life for a friend? I hope the meaning of this passage will sink into your heart and be visible through your life as you go about your day-to-day business. Imagine a world where each Christian loves others as Christ loves them. Isn't it a beautiful picture?

Philippians 2:1-11

If you have any encouragement from being united with Christ, if any comfort from his love, if any fellowship with the Spirit, if any tenderness and compassion, then make my joy complete by being like-minded, having the same love, being one in spirit and purpose. Do nothing out of selfish ambition or vain conceit, but in humility consider others better than yourselves. Each of you should look not only to your own interests, but also to the interests of others. Your attitude should be the same as that of Christ Jesus: Who, being in very nature God, did not consider equality with God something to be grasped, but made himself nothing, taking the very nature of a servant, being made in human likeness. And being found in appearance as a man, he humbled himself and became obedient to death-- even death on a cross! Therefore God exalted him to the highest place and gave him the name that is above every name, that at the name of Jesus every knee should bow, in heaven and on earth and under the earth, and every tongue confess that Jesus Christ is Lord, to the glory of God the Father. (NIV)

What does Christian love look like in this passage?

How does God expect us to show love to our Christian sisters and brothers?

What parts of this passage give you trouble?

I always find these glimpses into God's viewpoint enlightening. When we have a chance to see how he wants us to behave toward one another, I always contrast it with how the world expects us to act. How many worldly leaders would say: "Put the other guy first and think of yourself second?" None that I can think of.

But this is what God expects of us. Want to show God you love him? Show love to the people he puts in your path: think of them first, be compassionate, be humble, work with them for God's purposes. These don't sound like impossible tasks, do they? They're not always easy, but God never promised us easy, did he?

One important piece of this puzzle is learning to become like Christ – not trying to put ourselves on equal footing with God but striving to please him in all things. This is at the heart of the life Jesus lived here on the earth. He did all things to please the Father, and he never put himself on equal footing with God, even though he is the Word, the Son of God who was with God in the beginning and spoke all things into being.

If Jesus didn't consider equality with God something he needed to have, why do we behave like God's equals? Why do we question his motives, doubt his word, or think we know better? If we want to become Christ-like, we must acknowledge that God is the ultimate authority. His word will guide us in all we do and show us how to live, but we have to give ourselves to him completely.

God has given us the most precious gift – his love. He trusts us as his children to turn around and use it on others. Think of how many people in this world need to know how much God loves them. How many people are walking around this world with a hole in their heart that only God can fill?

1 Corinthians 13

If I speak in the tongues of men and of angels, but have not love, I am only a resounding gong or a clanging cymbal. If I have the gift of prophecy and can fathom all mysteries and all knowledge, and if I have a faith that can move mountains, but have not love, I am nothing. If I give all I possess to the poor and surrender my body to the flames, but have not love, I gain nothing. Love is patient, love is kind. It does not envy, it does not boast, it is not proud. It is not rude, it is not self-seeking, it is not easily angered, it keeps no record of wrongs. Love does not delight in evil but rejoices with the truth. It always protects, always trusts, always hopes, always perseveres. Love never fails. But where there are prophecies, they will cease; where there are tongues, they will be stilled; where there is knowledge, it will pass away. For we know in part and we prophesy in part, but when perfection comes, the imperfect disappears. When I was a child, I talked like a child, I thought like a child, I reasoned like a child. When I became a man, I put childish ways behind me. Now we see but a poor reflection as in a mirror; then we shall see face to face. Now I know in part; then I shall know fully, even as I am fully known. And now these three remain: faith, hope and love. But the greatest of these is love. (NIV)

What does this passage say to you?

Why do you think love is so important?

What is the effect of good things done without love?

Do you get any mental picture in your mind based on Paul's description of love? If so, what do you see?

I think this is the perfect passage to end our study with. He spells everything out simply for us. We can do the most wonderful things in the world, but if we do them without love it means nothing. We are nothing without love. Think about that for a moment. We can possess everything in the world, but without love it's nothing. We can give up everything we possess – even our life – but without love it means nothing. I guess God thinks love is kind of important, huh?

Look at God's picture of love for a moment. We have a long list of things love isn't and a short list of things love is. Let's look at those lists.

Love isn't: envious, boastful, proud, rude, self-seeking, easily angered, grudge-holding, or evil embracing. You can get a clear picture of what love shouldn't look like by reading the list above.

Fortunately for us, Paul also gives us a descriptive list of what love should look like. Love is: patient, kind, protecting, trusting, hopeful, persevering, and never-failing. Look at these two lists for a moment. Which one personifies most relationships in your life? Which one personifies how you love?

God has given each one of us the ability to love others as he loves us. Does that mean it's a foregone conclusion that Christians are going to love others this way? Of course not.

Unfortunately, we can choose to love any way we want to, and we often choose incorrectly. We choose to love based on criteria that we set up ourselves, or let the world choose our criteria for us. We love our spouses until it's hard to, then we let them go. We love our friends until they disagree with us, then we cut them loose. We love God when things are going well and trouble's not knocking on our door, but at the first sign of hardship, we turn around and blame him for everything. That's not how he would have us love.

With God's love first in our hearts, we learn to forgive spouses when things go wrong; we learn to give and take with friends and work problems out; we learn to praise God in the good times and hold on tight to his hand when things go wrong. That's loving as God loves us, and that's the love that will conquer all.

Concluding Remarks

I think Paul's words in Ephesians 3:16-21 provide an excellent conclusion to this lesson.

He says, *"I pray that out of his glorious riches he may strengthen you with power through his Spirit in your inner being, so that Christ may dwell in your hearts through faith. And I pray that you, being rooted and established in love, may have power, together with all the saints, to grasp how wide and long and high and deep is the love of Christ, and to know this love that surpasses knowledge--that you may be filled to the measure of all the fullness of God. Now to him who is able to do immeasurably more than all we ask or imagine, according to his power that is at work within us, to him be glory in the church and in Christ Jesus throughout all generations, for ever and ever! Amen."*

Can you grasp how wide and long and high and deep Christ's love is for you? The mental picture this passage provides is a love too big for any of us to imagine. We are so loved, sisters, and I want you to feel that love in your life each and every day. That love should pour out of each one of us and draw others to our God and his endless supply of it.

Challenge

Your final challenge is this: Love. I want you to take what you have learned in this lesson and put it into real practice in your life. Work on loving your family like the Proverbs 31 Woman loved hers. Love everyone around you like Christ loves you. **Journal about your experiences here.**

Wrapping It Up

I hope that the Proverbs 31 Woman is less intimidating to you now. She is someone we each should consider a friend and mentor, especially now that we've learned about the characteristics that make her a great wife, mother, and woman. If you're still feeling overwhelmed by her, remember that every person is a work in progress. Keep working toward the goal!

Let's review her list one more time together. You might find it helpful to tack this list up somewhere in your home so you can remind yourself to work on any of the virtues that are giving you trouble.

A Proverbs 31 Woman is:
- A woman who fears the Lord
- Self-controlled and virtuous
- Responsible
- Kind and compassionate
- Hardworking and resourceful
- Energetic
- Wise
- Loved by her God

With an active prayer life, help from fellow Christians, and persistence, you can change your life for the positive and live as a woman who fears the Lord.

Group Wrap-Up

Group Goals

Did your group meet the goals set at the beginning of the study? Why or why not?

What progress have you seen on your beginning prayer requests?

Personal Goals

Did you find what you were looking for personally? If not, what stopped you?

What area(s) of your life do you still need God's help with?

Did this study help you with the personal struggles you were having? If so, how did it help? If not, what was missing?

About the Author

Amanda Peterson is a wife and mom who loves living near the beach. After a forced "retirement" from personal training due to back injuries, she turned to writing as a way to contribute to her family and maintain her sanity. She writes books for children and ladies' Bible studies, and she also leads the studies with her faithful group of women. Visit her on the web at: www.amandarpeterson.blogspot.com.

Amanda loves to hear from readers. Send her an email at: amandap3311@gmail.com with any comments or questions on this study.

20788018R00096

Made in the USA
Middletown, DE
08 June 2015